Be Your Own Saju Master: A Primer of the Four Pillars Method

This is a much-awaited guide to examine one's life journey through a set of ancient wisdom. As a companion to astrological charts and a supplementary to spiritual quests, the book helps to (re)open various chapters of our lives. There is a saying that people teach who they are. The book embodies multiple aspects of who the author is: teacher, counselor, pastor, lover, writer, and cultural translator. The author testifies in this book how sajuology can help uncover the intersectional and messy identities in life.
Jung Ha Kim, PhD, author of *Religions in Asian America, Singing the Lord's Song in a New Land* and *Bridge-Makers and Cross-Bearers*

I am recommending this book because there is no other book like this where you can learn to read your saju chart in a step-by-step way, in English. The book provides deep insights and the tools to help learners dive deeper into understanding themselves, their families, and the key elements for healing and growth. Nothing is ever set in stone in life, but by understanding our Four Pillars, we can use the information to help transform our lives in a positive way.
Judy Yi, instructor and practitioner of pranic healing

The challenges for books on saju are always the translation that seems to be either too technical or too watered down where you cannot even recognize the original intent. Dr Kim has written a masterpiece where she holds the tension between scholarly integrity and readability for the novice. Dr Kim's labor of love in the book comes out through and through. I enthusiastically recommend it.
David D. Kim, PhD, author and founder/CEO of Research Institute for Counseling Education (RICE)

Disclaimer

The information in this book is presented to the best of the author's knowledge. The author and the publisher have made their best efforts to produce this book to serve as a helpful guide. They make no guarantees regarding the accuracy or the completeness of the information contained herein, and accept no responsibility or liability for any losses or damages caused or alleged to be caused from using the information offered in this book.

Be Your Own Saju Master: A Primer of the Four Pillars Method

Decode Your Saju Chart to Unearth Your Subconscious Where Your Future and Destiny Are on the Make

Be Your Own Saju Master: A Primer of the Four Pillars Method

Decode Your Saju Chart to Unearth Your Subconscious Where Your Future and Destiny Are on the Make

Sarah Kim

BOOKS

Winchester, UK
Washington, USA

JOHN HUNT PUBLISHING

First published by O-Books, 2024
O-Books is an imprint of John Hunt Publishing Ltd., 3 East St., Alresford,
Hampshire SO24 9EE, UK
office@jhpbooks.com
www.johnhuntpublishing.com
www.o-books.com

For distributor details and how to order please visit the 'Ordering' section on our website.

ISBN: 978 1 80341 418 8
978 1 80341 419 5 (ebook)
Library of Congress Control Number: 2022919127

A CIP catalogue record for this book is available from the British Library.

Design: Lapiz Digital Services

UK: Printed and bound by CPI Group (UK) Ltd, Croydon, CR0 4YY
Printed in North America by CPI GPS partners

The author of this book does not dispense medical advice or
prescribe the use of any technique as a form of treatment for
physical, emotional, or medical problems without the advice of a
physician, either directly or indirectly. The intent of the author
is only to offer information of a general nature to help you in
your quest for emotional and spiritual well-being. In the event
you use any of the information in this book for yourself, which is
your constitutional right, the author and the publisher assume no
responsibility for your actions.

We operate a distinctive and ethical publishing philosophy in
all areas of our business, from our global network of authors to
production and worldwide distribution.

To my family

Contents

Preface

In the fall of 2004, I began my residency at the local counseling center in Atlanta as a doctoral student studying pastoral care and counseling. I counseled clients from diverse backgrounds who sought help with issues concerning relationships, life style, money, health, and future prospects. The clients represented different races, ethnicities, cultures, religions, and gender identities, and yet the methods used to serve them homogeneously derived from Western psychology and variations of psychotherapeutic techniques. Naturally, my colleagues and professors were keen on developing counseling methods equipped with cultural sensitivity, which gave the contextuality of the counseling situation a new, broader meaning.

I completed the program with a dissertation titled *Spirituality of Awareness*. This was the culmination of my research on Eastern practices that inform about wholeness and the ways to achieve it. In Buddhism, for instance, the experiential event of Enlightenment is deemed as the ultimate path to wholeness by liberating the human individual from suffering itself. To this, the Swiss psychoanalyst Carl G. Jung commented, "We need suffering. Without it, life is no longer interesting" (*Self and Liberation*, Meckel & Moore, 1992). Jung was well versed in and influenced by Buddhism, and his comment highlighted the tension between the ideal and the practical—in our quest for healing and wholeness. During my research years, I had participated in a meditation program in the foothills of Mt Gyeryong, known as the spiritual mountain of South Korea. After 13 hours of sitting meditation every day for a week, I had reached a state of profound lightness of being that generated feelings of joy from within. I was simply and genuinely content, not for any particular reason; but the feelings eventually faded when the effects of meditation diminished. We may envy the monks in the temples and the saints in the monasteries who live a life of meditation and prayer by vocation, but the majority of us are destined to live in the secular world and attend to the vicissitudes of life. Life is not a walk in the park, and we need a practical guide to get through it.

The Four Pillars method has been that guide for me and the multitude of others who are familiar with its utility and value. The method helps us to understand others by shedding light on the person's inner world and his or her external circumstances. It offers a compelling perspective on the dynamics of interpersonal relationships. It explains our past, and predicts the general path of our life's journey. It helps us to make informed decisions about our life's affairs.

When I began studying sajuology (saju is the Korean term for Four Pillars) about 17 years ago, the textual research involved delving into older and newer books written in Korean that were studded with archaic Chinese characters that originate from ancient texts on the subject. (The language is part of the reason why saju studies is considered a difficult undertaking.) After getting through all the books I can get my hands on, I was eager to learn from the masters and listen to their scholarly views and stories of practice. I met and learned from several teachers in Korea, and I was astonished by the differences in the methodologies they used. One saju master, who was a former politician, had used his influence to access one thousand medical records of random individuals in order to examine the correlation between a person's saju composition and the disease he or she had. It seemed to be a unique way of gathering information, and I was impressed by his dedication to research.

As an ancient divination art form, the Four Pillar method and its literary legacy have been carried on by a very small group of people from each generation. I have joined that group because

I believe in the practical value of the method of helping people who are seekers at heart. If you are standing in the middle of darkness about any aspect of your life, and need a guiding light, you have come to the right place.

Be Your Own Saju Master is a product of years of textual and contextual research, and it contains the distilled wisdom I have gained from spending countless hours of saju consultation with individuals, couples, and families. To help readers engage with the learning material, I have consistently focused on clarity and conciseness throughout the book. I did not include the more complex set of theories in this primer, so learners can set their footing firmly on the foundational theories. The advanced theories will be introduced in a sequel volume. It is my prayer and hope that you will be enriched by the reading experience.

Acknowledgments

This book has come to fruition with the help and support of many special individuals in my life. With deep gratitude and appreciation, I thank:

***

All my clients for sharing their lives with me; you have been an invaluable source of inspiration and learning.

***

The teachers and the spiritual leaders I have learned from; you have shown faith in me so that I could make this literary contribution.

***

My friends and colleagues who have supported me through the years of research and the writing process, especially David, Nami, Jungha, and Judy, for their encouragement and timely advices.

***

The publishing team at John Hunt Publishing for their openness to novel ideas and their exceptional work in making this book come to life.

***

Acknowledgments

My son, Jonathan, for reading the first draft of the manuscript and giving me helpful feedback.

***

And my husband, Andrew, for supporting me with love and patience, and for always being there.

Introduction

Human life is essentially tied to the concept of time. Our birth and death and everything else in between are defined by time. This is true for all individuals who are destined to live through a certain segment of time unique to their existence. If a single moment in time is a piece of thread, the entire segment can be seen as a fabric having distinctive texture and design. This book is about the very fabric of time that defines and sustains individual destiny. Realizing one's destiny involves an understanding of time as one's own existential context.

The content introduced in this volume is a primer of saju philosophy, or sajuology. Sajuology is widely known as the Four Pillars philosophy; it refers to the body of knowledge surrounding the theory of human nature and destiny that bases its premise on the natural scientific data linked to the human life cycles. Saju literally means "four pillars," and though it is pronounced differently around the world, I am using the Korean pronunciation of the two Han characters representing the term: 四柱 (sah-joo). The term "saju" is used interchangeably with the term "Four Pillars" throughout the book.

Rooted in ancient wisdom of the Far East, sajuology comes with its own set of language and symbols. One of the challenging aspects of planning to write this book has been about deciding what to translate and what to keep in the original form. I have made conscious efforts to deliver what appears to be a complex, systematic literature in an approachable manner without diminishing its scholarly authenticity. As a result, I have translated everything except for the twenty-two Han characters of the Saju Alphabet that constitute the building blocks of the Four Pillars. I have refrained from reducing the original alphabet to a set of natural elements or animal symbols.

Knowing the actual alphabet in Han characters will enable the learner to construct, read, and analyze any saju chart.

四柱

sa·ju

Four Pillars

Learning the basic tenets of sajuology may come across as easy or difficult depending on your learning objectives. Like learning a new language, it takes memorization and analytical skills. It takes patience and an open mind. Learning the theories is probably the easier first step; applying the theories in real life situations by engaging the interpretative process tends to be more challenging — as we must exercise care and humility in respect for the sacredness of individual lives. Ultimately, achieving proficiency in the discipline will depend on the learner's desire and will power. It would be wise to have faith in your learning, to trust the process, and to take your time. I recommend that you keep your own saju chart next to you as you explore the contents of the following chapters. This will motivate you to engage the learning material on the personal level. The basic principles of the Four Pillars method are organized into fifteen chapters in this book. This is the basic information that a learner must have in order to read and analyze the saju charts.

My goal in introducing sajuology to the English-speaking audience is two-fold: 1) To transmit a historically and culturally significant body of knowledge that comes with practical wisdom for enhancing people's lives; and 2) to help learners to attain the interpretation skills needed to apply the knowledge in real life settings. I am aware that saju reading practices are often misconstrued either as doubtful fortune telling or esoteric knowledge of a few specially gifted people. I hope to abate these misconceptions by providing accessible and accurate information about sajuology. The Protestant Reformation leader, Martin Luther, once said, "Peace if possible; truth at all costs." The truth is like a shining light, and it has a way of making its presence known even through the tiniest crevice. It is about time that more people come to see the light concerning the ways of realizing their destiny.

Chapter 1 The Context

Between stimulus and response there is a space. In that space is our power to choose our response. In our response lies our growth and our freedom.
Victor E. Frankl

In sajuology, your time in this world begins with the first breath you take outside of your mother's womb. (The month of your conception inside the womb is noted, but is not used in saju evaluation.) Life unfolds before our eyes from this point and on, calling us to choose in moments of truth, and to choose wisely if it can be helped. Victor Frankl's notion of the liminal space between stimulus and response is something we live through every day, though it rarely crosses our minds, unless we are about to make a choice that will have a lasting impact on our lives. Consider a divorcee seeking a second chance in marriage, a college student choosing a career path, a lifetime homemaker who wants to start a new venture in business, and an accomplished professional trying to keep a balance between a demanding job and health stricken with serious illness. These people have one thing in common: Their liminal space is filled with anxiety from uncertainty as they do not know what their choice will bring. In such cases, divination can offer help. Divination is as old as time, even older than organized religion. Our desire to transcend the mundane world is like an impulse embedded in the human DNA; and our desire to reach the ultimate truth—about the world and about ourselves—has generated volumes of divinatory methods over the course of human civilization throughout the ages. Sajuology is one of these methods originating from the East Asian context.

In the dominant cultures, Asian or not, the practice of evaluating one's saju is often tainted by the stigma of being superstitious. People are curious to hear about their fortune, but a sense of "mixed feelings" is usually attached to their curiosity, because they are entirely vulnerable when it comes to judging the accuracy of the evaluation. They simply have to live to find out the outcome of their inquiry over time. Thus, having trust in the saju reader is an important issue during an evaluation. How, then, do you know whom to trust? This is hard to say, because there are no institutional bodies that license the readers with an official stamp of approval. You more or less have to rely on the reader's reputation or a friend's recommendation. If you're in luck, you may find the reading quite helpful; in the worst-case scenario, it could turn out to be a waste of time and money.

So, the stigma is not all that unwarranted. The problem, in my view, has to do with the incompetencies of the practitioners who misguide or misinform their clients even if it is done unwittingly. Some of them appear to take the practice superstitiously themselves, telling the client to "take it lightly since it's just for fun." The worst kind are those who outright lie for monetary gain. One must also beware of those who focus on the negativities to the point of depriving the client of any hope, instilling fear and anxiety. Anything seems possible in the world of the free market, but selling advice to people about their life and destiny should come with caution and prudence within the boundaries of professional ethics.

Our societies need more proficient and respectable practitioners working to help people. What would be even better is that people become skilled saju readers themselves by learning the tenets of sajuology. While this may be easier said than done, information in this book is designed to help serious learners to become skillful in saju interpretation to a meaningful degree. It is best to begin with your saju chart and the charts of your loved ones. Expect to confront questions and unsureness. If you do not give up, there will be an aha moment as you begin to understand your life's journey and your interpersonal relationships on the deeper level.

The shortcomings of a few practitioners should not be a reflection on the theory itself, however. The Four Pillars system is a product of intellectual and empirical inquiries just like any other theory that has enlightened humanity. The dictionary defines superstition as "a widely held but unjustified belief in supernatural causation." Sajuology is not about practicing superstition; it is neither unjustified nor does it adhere to supernatural causation. Its theoretical origins, in fact, heavily relied on the laws of nature. Sajuology can be categorized in the domain of natural sciences—natural anthropology, to be specific. From the laws of nature derived the theories on human nature and destiny, establishing the basis for sajuological praxis. The beauty of any theory is in its power to explain and to predict. The culmination of sajuology as a theory lies in its capacity to offer explanations and predictions about an individual's life, relationships, and destiny.

The laws of nature introduced in this book are simple and appeal to the common senses. The secret to achieving success and happiness in life starts with recognizing this simplicity and yielding to the ways of nature. In our respect for and cooperation with nature, we also recognize that we are part of nature. We must see that nature is in us and that we are in nature. This is the message of the Four Pillars philosophy—that we realize our individual potential in life by recognizing and claiming the wondrous gift of nature we are born with.

The Beginning

The literature on saju studies branched out from one of the oldest texts on the art of divination—the *I Ching*, or *The Book of Change.* As a widely recognized classical text of China, the *I Ching* is more than just a book—it is an invention, a hallmark of human intellectual achievement dating back some five thousand years. *The Book of Change* is known to reveal the reality of everything, and has given birth to other disciplines that have advanced the Eastern civilization. The great Chinese scholar Confucius said near the end of his life: "If the heavens allowed a few more years of life in me, I would avoid a great error by finishing my study of *I Ching.*" Confucius encountered the *I Ching* at age 50 and discovered that it contained the answers he had been seeking all his life, but he knew he didn't have enough time to master the book to his satisfaction. The *I Ching* is written in archaic Han characters, and even the most erudite scholars had difficulty understanding its contents. The book demanded the learner's time and effort in deciphering the characters encoded with layers of revelations about nature and human beings.

The Eight Symbols of *I Ching*

Over time, the foundational principles of *I Ching* have shaped the collective unconscious of Asian people. Having survived the test of time and marking its theoretical significance on multiple disciplines, the *I Ching* is built on one fundamental truth: Change is the essence of life, and all things are changing all the time. The book is all about the dynamics of change, as revealed by its title. The writers of *I Ching* relied on their experience and observations of the natural world and discovered the cyclical patterns of change—the mysterious regularity that repeats itself throughout the space-time continuum. The irony in this is the discovery of the constant by the way of change. In other words, the only constant known to humanity is *change* and the *cyclical patterns of change* as experienced and witnessed by humans.

A Brief History of Sajuology in Northeast Asia

The earliest texts on the Four Pillars system that are known to most resemble what is being used today were, purportedly, developed by the Chinese scholars from the Tang (618-907 CE) through the Song (960-1279 CE) dynasties. The development of saju studies in Korea appeared around 1392 with the emergence of the Chosun dynasty. In Japan, saju scholarship took a definitive form and prestige toward the end of the Edo period in the early nineteenth century, based on the works of a Japanese scholar dedicated to Confucianism. The intellectual roots of the Four Pillar system are common among the three countries, but each country had its own emphasis and style. The Chinese took on a mathematical approach by calling the Four Pillars method in terms of *calculating* human destiny. The method is more popularly known as Chinese Astrology in China and abroad. The Japanese used a rational approach by framing the method as an *inference* of human destiny. The Koreans embraced a scholarly approach by naming it the *principles* of human destiny. In these contexts, the Four Pillars philosophy is not so much a superstitious fortunetelling that depends on random chances, but it employs a practical methodology that involves conceptual analysis of the theories pertaining to the laws of nature.

In summary, sajuology is a practical discipline stemming from the timeless culture of divination with a minimum of thirteen hundred years of developmental history in the Northeast Asian region. While the theoretical emphases and nomenclature may vary in different cultural settings, the Four Pillars evaluation practice served, and continues to serve, the singular purpose of helping people to understand and manage their life and destiny.

Chapter 2 Anatomy of Saju

It is not in the stars to hold our destiny but in ourselves.
William Shakespeare

To construct a saju chart, it is crucial to use the accurate date and the hour of birth of the querent. As a theory that offers roadmaps of individual destiny, sajuology is profoundly concerned with the dimension of time. When we consider change as the essence of life, the notion of time is unavoidable since change always occurs over time. Human conception, birth, aging, and death distinctively follow a timeline. Our whole life is intricately woven in the fabric of time that gives us context and meaning. As a concept, time represents the continued sequence of our existence. It gives us a sense of the past, the present, and the future. We reflect on our past from memory; we live the present through the sensory faculties; and we anticipate the future in hope and imagination. Time is quantifiable, which makes it possible to organize our life patterns—everything we do, including sleep, work, eating, and playing, is done in relation to time.

An important discovery in modern science is the understanding that time cannot be viewed apart from space. Stephen Hawking makes this point in *A Brief History of Time*: "We must accept that time is not completely separate from and independent of space, but is combined with it to form an object called space-time." So, then, what does space represent? In the larger context, space refers to the universe that is in motion since the event of its birth, the Big Bang. In the immediate context, the earth is the space that concerns us. According to the *I Ching*, time is *yang* in character given its metaphysical nature. Time is invisible and impalpable, yet it is absolutely consequential to every aspect of human life. Space, on the other hand, is deemed *yin* by nature since it comes in physical, tangible forms. In line with the scientific claim, sajuology informs us that combining time and space generates a complete, harmonious yin-yang unity.

Before Albert Einstein introduced the theory of relativity, space and time were thought to be absolute, fixed entities. The theory of relativity suggested that the space-time continuum is rather dynamic, equipped with its own *curvature* that can both affect and be affected by the changes happening in its surroundings. This means that every planet has its own measure of time that depends on the movements of the nearby planets, including the almighty sun.

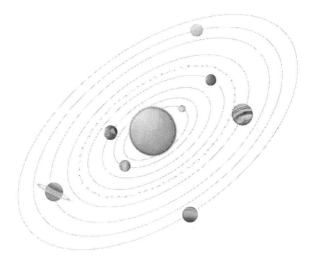

Since ancient times, human ancestors looked to the sky to measure time on Earth. The 24-hour day was conceptualized according to the phenomena of sunrise and sunset, the 4-week long months according to the changing shape of the moon, and the 12-month long year according to the repetitious cycle of the four seasons. Time on Earth, as such, is linked to the changes we observe in nature, namely the astronomical observations that opened the doors to astrological interpretations.

The Four Pillars

The Four Pillars in the saju chart represent the year, month, day, and hour of one's birth. The Four Pillars method is built on the premise that the precise time you were born has something to say about your life and destiny. A saju can forecast the querent's path in life, including her family of origin, significant relationships, psychological state of mind, personality, education, career path, health issues, wealth, and more. Similar to how our biological DNA determines our physical manifestation over time, a saju is encoded with information on how our destiny is likely to unfold in a lifetime. The accuracy of the forecasts range between 60 to 90 percent, and there is no such thing as 100 percent accuracy in terms of predictability. Human destiny is not about determinism. Nothing is set in stone. We must respect the small percentage of unknowability that offers room for individual free will, religious faith, and divine intervention to shape and influence the outcome of our lives.

In the saju chart, the Year, Month, Day, and Hour Pillars can be lined up from left to right or from right to left. This is a matter of the saju reader's preference. In the olden days of the Eastern world, words were written from right to left, so the Four Pillars were lined up with the Year Pillar on the far right and the Hour Pillar on the far left. I am using this set up throughout the book.

Hour	Day	Month	Year

The Four Pillars of a Saju Chart

The importance of using an accurate birth information cannot be overstated when constructing the saju chart. You must use the date and the hour of your actual birth. Some people have inaccurate birth dates printed on their personal documents for various reasons, and if this is the case, it is best to double check with someone—such as your parents—who can verify the birth information. If you do not know your accurate birth date and if there is no way to verify the information, your saju chart, unfortunately, could not be established.

If the birth hour is the only thing that cannot be verified, saju reading is still possible, though the retrievable information may be reduced due to the missing Hour Pillar. Some saju readers try to insert every hour of the clock in the Hour Pillar to see if the analysis matches the querent's actual life, but this approach can be time-consuming and potentially misleading in determining the actual birth hour.

Here is an example of a birthdate and the birth location:

August 29, 1958 7:33 PM
Gary, Indiana USA

This birth information is from the solar (Gregorian) calendar we use every day. It belongs to a well-known twentieth-century pop singer, Michael Jackson. In order to convert the birthdate into an analyzable saju chart, we must now consult the Ten-Thousand-Year (TTY) calendar.

About the Ten-Thousand-Year (TTY) Calendar

The TTY calendar traditionally contained the lunar dates only, but the modern printed versions conveniently come with the corresponding solar dates of the Gregorian calendar. If you come from a culture that normally uses the lunar calendar, you will need to verify whether the birthdate you know is from the lunar or the solar calendar. Do not assume that your birthdate is from the solar calendar; your parents may have used your lunar birthdate on your official documents, as this is a common practice in many Asian cultures. Be careful not to evaluate a wrong saju chart by doing your research to obtain the accurate birth information to work with.

A Modern Version of the TTY Calendar

Today, several websites offer Four Pillars calculating tools where you can insert your birthdate to instantly pull up your saju chart. In the past, a saju reader's must-have item was a thick, phonebook-sized TTY calendar; without the calendar, he could not construct a saju chart no matter how brilliant he might be in analyzing it.

A Saju Calculator at www.saju-clinic.com/sajucalculator.html

The TTY calendar has existed for thousands of years and is currently in use across the globe. It offers more information than a simple lunar calendar in that it contains sets of Han characters from the Sexagenary Cycle to indicate the dates. The two Han characters—whether they represent the year, month, day, or hour—are stacked with the first character (Stem) on the top and the second character (Branch) on the bottom, forming a vertical pillar. (The two characters can also be written horizontally.) The TTY calendar is traditionally referred to as the Stem-Branch calendar. Hence, when the Four Pillars are established, the saju chart automatically comes with eight Han characters. A saju is also called *sa-ju-pal-ja* (四柱八字), meaning "four-pillars-eight-characters." Pal-Ja, which is the shorter term often used to refer to one's saju, is equivalent to the Chinese term, Ba Zi.

The Entertainer's Saju

From the TTY calendar, we are able to construct Michael Jackson's saju chart. The birth hour of 6:33pm is used instead of the recorded hour of 7:33pm since his birthdate falls on daylight saving time based on his birth location. (Daylight saving time was set by artificially adding an hour to the actual time, so in saju reading practice, one hour needs to be subtracted.)

Hour	Day	Month	Year
辛	戊	庚	戊
shin yin metal	*moo* yang earth	*kyoung* yang metal	*moo* yang earth
酉	寅	申	戌
yoo yin metal	*inn* yang wood	*shin* yang metal	*sool* yang earth

Michael Jackson's Four Pillars

Jackson was born in the year of the Golden Dog (戊戌), on the month of the White Monkey (庚申), on the day of the Golden Tiger (戊寅), in the hour of the White Rooster (辛酉). The primary element representing his "Self" is the 戊 Moo Earth (top character, Day Pillar) that is surrounded by four Metals standing next to it from both sides—庚, 申, 辛, 酉. Both the Month and the Hour Pillars in the chart are entirely made up of Metals. From the 戊 Moo Earth (Self)'s position, the four Metals represent "Outputs," and from this many Outputs in the saju, we can surmise that work had disproportionately dominated the singer's life. From an early age to the end of his life, Jackson produced and performed music—his destined art form—on the prolific level. Meanwhile, the 寅 Inn Wood (bottom character, Day Pillar) seeks to control the 戊 Moo Earth (Self) above it, attributing to the perfectionist tendency of the singer, especially when it comes to his work. The 寅 Inn Wood, however, appears to be threatened by all the Metals surrounding it. Hence, the owner of this saju is likely to experience health issues along with relationship and marital problems on a notable level.

This is a sample of how a saju chart is constructed and interpreted. Once you learn the basic concepts of the Four Pillars system in the following chapters, you will become more familiar with the task. You needn't be alarmed by the seeming complexity of the Han characters making up the Four Pillars as there are only twenty-two characters to learn. Decoding and analyzing the characters is an intriguing process once you grasp the theoretical basics. There are layers of information to be unearthed from each character and from combinations of characters. In a time-limited saju consultation session, it is helpful to focus on a few pertinent pieces of information that matter the most to you for the time being. The amount of information that can be retrieved from a saju chart and the accompanying luck cycles simply cannot be discussed fully in a one-hour setting. Evaluating your saju can be a one-time deal or an ongoing routine. In saju reading cultures, reading once a year is the norm, since a new year always brings a new luck cycle that can impact your personal luck for better or worse. You will be able to determine this for yourself once you complete learning the contents of the following chapters.

***

Chapter 2 Exercise

1. Construct your saju chart using an online TTY Calendar (Saju Calculator).
2. Construct the saju chart(s) of your significant other(s).

Chapter 3 The Day Master

If you know your destiny, you wouldn't blame God for what you get in life. If you know who you are as a person, you wouldn't blame others for what you get in relationships.
An Old Chinese Proverb

In the saju chart, the Day Pillar is a special pillar, because it represents the Self, the saju owner. While the Day Pillar as a whole offers the quickest way to make an assessment concerning one's character and temperament, the Heavenly Stem (the top character) occupying the Day Pillar is viewed as the Self, and the entire saju chart is interpreted from the viewpoint of the Self. The Heavenly Stem in the Day Pillar is hence called the "Day Master." The other Pillars—Year, Month, and Hour—present the general living environment of the Self. These Pillars and their characters have a *relationship* with the Day Master, which generates analytical implications.

The Earthly Branch portion (the bottom character) of the Day Pillar symbolizes the physical body of the Self or the person very close to the Self such as a spouse—the Self's other half. Designating the Heavenly Stem as the Self translates to an emphasis on the metaphysical existence of the Self as in one's spirit, mind, or soul; our physical body is deemed secondary to the metaphysical energy that animates it. As Pierre Teilhard de Chardin put it, "We are not human beings having a spiritual experience. We are spiritual beings having a human experience."

Hour	Day	Month	Year
	The Day Master (Self)		

There exists no clear explanation as to why the Heavenly Stem of the Day Pillar is deemed as the Self. The concept of the Day Master simply has been an integral aspect of sajuology ever since it was first introduced by a scholar in the name of Seo Jah Pyong (徐子平) of China's Song Dynasty, who is considered the architect of the current version of the Four Pillars system widely being used today. Using the Day Master concept is thus traditionally called the "Jah Pyong Method." The concept has persisted through the centuries as a central theory in saju studies because it continues to prove its theoretical validity within the analytical framework. In defense of Jah Pyong's theory, I believe it makes sense to use the Day Stem to represent the Self. The time frame suggested by the Year or the Month Pillar is too stretched out, and the time frame covered by the Hour Pillar is too short to define the individual. The Day Pillar is the best option left to represent the individual. In a 24-hour period of a day, a person fully experiences the yin-yang energies of day and night, undergoes the biorhythmic changes through consumption, excretion, active movements and sleep, engaging in the self-renewal process for the mind and the body. These daily regularities or cyclical patterns define the distinctive and multifaceted experience of the human individual in the time frame of a day. Moreover, a person's birthday is considered the most special day worthy of recognition and celebration across different cultures.

There is a good amount of literature on Chinese astrology that highlights the importance of the birth year. In these texts, the birth year in the form of an animal symbol takes the center stage in informing the person's character, temperament, and the list of harmonious combinations of animals for finding harmony in relationships. From the perspective of sajuology, the birth year in the animal symbol is just one character out of the eight that make up the Four Pillars. The Year Pillar undoubtedly offers analytical value in its own right, but it has its limitations in fully defining the individual. Focusing on just one character when you have seven additional ones to consider simply does not yield enough information about the person and his or her circumstances. We need to explore the Day Master and its surroundings to truly see and understand the person.

Let's explore a few examples of the Day Master:

***

January 8, 1942 10:08 AM / Oxford, England

Hour	Day	Month	Year
癸	辛	辛	辛
gyeh yin water	*shin* yin metal	*shin* yin metal	*shin* yin metal
巳	酉	丑	巳
sah yin fire	*yoo* yin metal	*chook* yin earth	*sah* yin fire

This saju belongs to the celebrity scientist Stephen Hawking. His Day Pillar indicates the Day Master as 辛 (*shin*), a yin metal element. The same characters are visible throughout the Year and the Month Pillars. The Earthly Branch (the bottom character) of the Day Pillar is a 酉 (*yoo*) Metal which is also a yin metal just like the Day Master. It is quite obvious that this saju composition possesses a great amount of yin metal energy, literally endowing Hawking with a mind of steel. (Metal is considered the toughest element.) The physical disability endured by the scientist never prevented him from actively using his mind to continue his research in physics and cosmology.

***

September 21, 1947 1:30 AM / Portland, Maine, US.

Hour	Day	Month	Year
癸	癸	己	丁
gyeh yin water	*gyeh* yin water	*ghee* yin earth	*jeong* yin fire
丑	卯	酉	亥
chook yin earth	*myo* yin wood	*yoo* yin metal	*hae* yin water

The above saju belongs to the famous novelist Stephen King. His Day Master in the Day Pillar is 癸 (*gyeh*) Water that is supported by the 卯 (*myo*) Wood underneath. A lot is going on throughout the Four Pillars, with Water and Fire clashing on the top row and Wood and Metal clashing on the bottom row. A reader might say that this saju indicates multiple challenges facing the Self. It seems that the author has succeeded in sublimating the clashing energies, by channeling them into his art of creative writing. His fiction genre is a natural fit for a saju that is dominant in yin energy.

***

July 1, 1961 2:30 PM / Norfolk, England

Hour	Day	Month	Year
癸	乙	甲	辛
gyeh yin water	*eul* yin wood	*gahp* yang wood	*shin* yin metal
未	未	午	丑
mee yin earth	*mee* yin earth	*oh* yang fire	*chook* yin earth

The above saju belongs to Diana Frances Spencer, the Princess of Wales. Her Day Master is 乙 (*eul*) Wood holding down the 未 (*mee*) Earth below. Surrounded by two fiery Earths and one Fire underneath, the Day Master longs for the support of its nurturer—water energy. The presence of 癸 (*gyeh*) Water in the Hour Pillar is therefore critical to the well-being of the Self. But, being a yin Water that is already challenged by multiple Earths surrounding it, its strength is limited in giving adequate support to the 乙 (*eul*) Wood Day Master, thus making this a hot and dry saju composition. The delicate 乙 (*eul*) Wood can constantly be challenged in such an environment. She died at the young age of 36 in a tragic car accident.

***

The three saju charts above share the dramatic and heroic lives of three notable public figures of modern history. We will revisit some of these saju compositions later when we discuss the interpretation tools and techniques.

***

Chapter 3 Exercise

1. Identify the Day Master in your saju chart. Identify its element and yin-yang energy.
2. Identify the Day Master in the saju chart(s) of your significant other(s).

Chapter 4 Forces of Yin and Yang

Great truth is a statement whose opposite is also a great truth.
Niels Bohr

In the *I Ching*, it is stated, "Once there is yang, and then once there is yin; this is the *dao*." A simple yet profound statement undergirding the foundation of *I Ching*'s worldview brings us to the concept of the yin-yang duality. When the Nobel laureate Niels Bohr received his knighthood—Denmark's highest honor—in 1947, he wore a coat-of-arms made with the yin-yang symbol and the Latin motto *contraria sunt complementa,* that translates to "opposites are complementary." It was an expression of his reverence for the *I Ching* and its principles, which culminated in his creation of the complementarity theory that dominated his thinking as a quantum physicist. Bohr enlightened the world with his atomic theory, where he showed the massive, positively charged nucleus (yang energy) orbited by the smaller, negatively charged electrons (yin energy) inside an atom, which strikingly resembled the heliocentric solar system.

The forces of yin and yang pervade all areas of existence from the smallest of an atom to the planetary system of which we are a part. Offering a lens to view the world in terms of its two categories, the yin-yang dualism makes a case for how the two entities relate to each other. The key word is alternation. The yin and the yang take their turns when it comes to occupying a segment of the space-time continuum.

The Yin-Yang Symbol

Figure 4.1

Consider the yin-yang symbol in Figure 4.1. The symbol has gained visibility in the West for several decades now, but little is known about the way it is designed. The symbol shows a circle that is loosely divided into white and black areas, with small eye-like circles of contrasting colors embedded in them. The original version of the symbol was first introduced in eleventh-century China, and later it was revised to take this simplified version. The original name for the figure is *taegeukdo* (太極圖), a term describing the vast span of the cosmos (太極 *taegeuk*) within a diagram (圖 *do*). The *taegeuk** concept, as reflected in the yin-yang symbol, conveys the following postulations:

The Infinite Void (無極)
The Yin is portrayed by the black shaded area in the symbol. It is known as the Infinite Void. This is considered as the state of Great Nothingness — the naturally existing universe in the form of static energy before anything was ever created. This is similar to the state of chaos before creation as narrated in the Bible: "a formless void and darkness." (Gen. 1:2) The Infinite Void, or Great Nothingness, is believed to be the state of the universe before the Big Bang.

The Great Absolute (太極)

The Yang is portrayed by the white shaded area in the symbol. In contrast to the Infinite Void that represents the chaotic nothingness, the Great Absolute represents order and function. It refers to the state of the universe in the form of dynamic energy from which all things were born. The universe is believed to have undergone four stages to reach this state: 1) the state of motionless (potential) energy, 2) the movement of energy, 3) the creation of forms, and 4) the function of forms. These stages suggest what the Big Bang process might have been like.

Meaning of the Smaller Circles

In Figure 4.1, there are two small circles with contrasting colors inside the two shades of black and white. The small circles symbolize the process of continual change, or transition, between the two opposite forces. They are the reminders that yin and yang do not exist apart from one another, but when the yang energy reaches its height, the yin energy begins to develop and expand in its place, and vice versa. And this cycle repeats itself continuously. This is in line with the law of conservation of energy that states, "energy can neither be created nor destroyed; it can only be transformed or transferred from one form to another." Energy in the universe as we know it is *constant* according to modern science, and it is continuously shifting, from one form (yin) to another (yang), resulting in the creative process that makes life sustainable. The changeability from one form of energy to the other once the former reaches its height is an important concept to remember when we engage in saju analysis. The continual transition between the yin and the yang forces comes as a result of the two energies' relentless tendency to reach a harmonious balance. One might say that there is a seed of yin in the yang, and a seed of yang in the yin, comparable to the notions of animus in a woman and anima in a man. Organisms can exist and maintain life because they are endowed with both energies of yin and yang.

***

SOUTH KOREA

* While *taegeuk* is a familiar concept in Eastern philosophy, South Korea is the only Asian country with its national flag embodying a depiction of *taegeuk* and the *I Ching* symbols.

Linguistic Origin

The Yin

The Han character for the word "yin" is a compilation of three Han characters with different meanings: 阝 (hill) + 今 (now) + 云 (cloud). The word portrays a place covered by the clouds.

The Yang

The Han character for the word "yang" is a compilation of the two Han characters with different meanings: 阝 (hill) + 昜 (rising sun). The word describes a place full of sun shining brightly.

The Characteristics of Yin and Yang

The yin and yang are generally defined as two different entities with opposing energies. Another way to understand the omnipresent duality is to view them in terms of relativity. The concept of relativity comes in handy when things aren't so black and white. For example, consider a man and a woman. Traditionally, the man belongs in the yang category and the woman in the yin. But what if the man is 5 feet tall and the woman is 6 feet in height? We can say that the man's smaller stature is *yin* in character in relation to the woman's larger stature that is, relatively speaking, *yang* in character. Adding to the complexity, the shorter man displays a quiet demeanor and likes to engage in contemplation in solitude—a yin personality. The taller woman is an extrovert who likes to be surrounded by people—a yang personality. So, which of the two individuals is closer to being yin or yang by comparison? This now becomes a judgment call. How one might judge, hence, depends on one's criteria for judgment.

The concept of relativity plays an important role in making judgments about categorizations. Here are some examples of what belongs in which category. Notice that certain things are categorized simply in relation to their opposing counterparts.

Yin

Moon, night, woman, darkness, ocean, low place, static, earth, autumn and winter, metal and water, cold, wet, weak, introvert, quiet, small, narrow, restraint, hide, even number, emptiness, decline, end, and death.

Yang

Sun, day, man, light, mountain, high place, dynamic, heaven, spring and summer, wood and fire, warm, dry, strong, extrovert, loud, large, wide, freedom, reveal, odd number, fullness, growth, beginning, and birth.

***

Chapter 4 Exercise

1. Examine the yin-yang energy distribution among the eight characters in your saju chart. Identify your dominant energy.
2. Examine the yin-yang energy distribution in the saju chart(s) of your significant other(s).

Chapter 5 The Five Phases/Elements

All things in the world come from being. And being comes from non-being.
Lao Tzu

Next to the yin-yang concept, the theory of the Five Phases comprises the overarching foundation of the Four Pillars method. The Yin-Yang and the Five Phases theories go hand-in-hand, like nuts and bolts, and burgers and fries. The Five Phases are called *phases* because of their non-static, dynamic nature, as they move from one phase to the next in continual sequence. At the same time, they possess natural properties as *elements*. In form, they possess properties of elements; in function, they move in phases. The two terms, Phases and Elements, will be used interchangeably throughout this book.

The Five Phases are the building blocks of the Four Pillars. A thorough understanding of the Five Phases and their dynamic — and dramatic — relationships is imperative for saju analysis. The Five Phases are: Wood, Fire, Earth, Metal, and Water. They represent the natural elements that make up this world, not just in the philosophical sense, but more so in the natural scientific sense, as the characteristics of each element are determined by the laws of nature.

In theory, the Five Phases are parented by the yin-yang duo. The creative energy culminated by the yin-yang union is known to generate the Five Elements, giving each element a visible form and a specific function. Put simply, it is the energy forces that precede the manifestation of material things. Energy and matter are, therefore, inseparable—just as parents and their children are genetically inseparable. The unity of energy and matter is a phenomenon seen all around us. Albert Einstein verified this with his famous equation: $E = mc^2$. In animate beings, energy comes in diverse forms. Humans are endowed with mental and spiritual energies in addition to the physical energy of the body. It is the unseen energy that begets the tangible matter, fulfilling its purpose through its fleshly vessel. This understanding gives a new light on the quote from the Lord's Prayer: "Thy will be done on earth, as it is in heaven." The heavens determine what happens on the earth.

Let's take a closer look at how the forces of yin and yang are manifested in the Five Phases. The Phases move in the sequence of Wood, Fire, Earth, Metal, and Water. They come in the order of their seasonal significance. Notice that the preceding phase always supports and promotes the following phase, creating a continuous, life-giving cycle.

The Five Elements/Phases

Wood

Wood represents the first energy among the Five Elements. Its designated color is green. Wood signifies the "Lesser Yang" depicted by the small white circle inside the black shaded area of the yin-yang symbol (Fig. 4.1). Wood is the byproduct of the interaction between Water and Fire. An example of this can be seen in the tropical region where hot temperatures (Fire) and rain and humidity (Water) host the perfect conditions for plants and trees to grow and thrive. Wood loves to grow; it can spread horizontally, but mostly, it loves to grow vertically, reaching out into the sky. The growing force is quite powerful, as it is moving against gravity. Wood thus is a natural leader with a competitive spirit and straightforwardness. Wood is also a nurturer, giving off warmth and inspiration, and providing shelter, shade, and fruits as life-giving resources for other living beings.

The Wood Phase

The Wood Phase represents the spring season, a time of birth and growth of life. It is a season of warmth, awakening the living from hibernation, out of the deadness of winter. This is a time of tremendous strength and force, as the smallest of a sprout can shoot through the icy hard wintry earth. In human stages of life, the Wood Phase signifies the period from birth through adolescence—the life segment marked by active growth and transformation. People with a saju that comes with a healthy amount of wood energy are likely to be warm, kind, nurturing, forthright, and equipped with leadership skills and positive attitude.

Fire

Fire represents the "Greater Yang," shown by the large white shaded area in the yin-yang symbol. Fire carries the color red.

Fire symbolizes the sun, the primary energy source for growth and development of life. The scripture introduces Fire in the form of light: "And God said, 'Let there be light,' and there was light. God saw that the light was good, and God separated the light from the darkness." (Gen. 1:3-4) Fire is associated with light, passion, vigorous energy, and openness that reveals and not hides. It also possesses great cleansing power just as Water does. Fire as an element tends to move upward, into the realm of heavens ruled by yang energy.

The Fire Phase

The preceding Wood Phase is the promoter of Fire. Fire as the second phase represents the summer season. It is a time when the sun is closest to the earth, soaking the earth and everything in it with massive energy of heat and light. In human life stages, the Fire Phase signifies the period from early to middle adulthood, the prime—the most productive and glorious— segment of life. A saju with a healthy amount of fire energy possesses the qualities of being passionate, energetic, open, expressive, and physically attractive.

Earth

Earth is the only element that is considered neutral. It is not categorized as yin or yang—though we will see later that Earth does come in yin and yang versions. Earth is expressed in the color yellow. Earth is symbolized by the large outer circle in the yin-yang symbol (Fig. 4.1). Earth is neutral because no other element can exist without the earth. Fire, Water, Metal, and Wood may come and go, but the earth always remains, accommodating life through the cycles of birth, growth, death, and rebirth. Earth is considered most active during the transitional periods when the seasonal energies are in active transition.

Being neutral, Earth is embedded, or hidden, in all of the other elements, and vice versa—meaning that Earth functions as a *storage* of other elements while other elements possess a trace of Earth in them. For instance, the earth transitioning from summer to autumn would have stored up the fire energy from the long, hot months of summer. This is a fiery earth—the earth that is in service of Fire; its function is to harbor and tame the accumulated fire energy so that the next season of autumn can unfold smoothly.

The Earth Phase

The neutral Earth is the third phase in order. The preceding Fire is the promoter of Earth; by warming up the earth, Fire makes it fertile and productive. The Earth Phase does not represent a season per se, but minds all four seasons, especially during the four transitional periods. The earth's activity during these transitions can be quite volatile—as in earthquakes, landslides, and volcanic activities. In human life stages, the Earth Phase represents the middle-ages, a place of plateau marked by stability and accumulated wealth and knowledge. (The potential for volatility still remains, as mid-life crises can occur during this period.)

Metal

Metal is the product of Earth, its nurturer. It holds the color white. Metal represents the "Lesser Yin," the small black circle inside the larger white area of the yin-yang symbol. Like Earth, it hardly moves or changes in form compared to Water or Fire. It doesn't grow like the way Wood does. Metal changes form only when a good amount of heat is applied. Metal symbolizes great strength given its tough, cool, sharp, and immobile characteristics.

The Metal Phase

The Metal Phase takes the fourth place in order. The preceding Earth Phase is the promoter of Metal. The Metal Phase represents the season of autumn, the beginning of yin energy for the year as the temperatures begin to drop. It is the time of harvest, lending words like "maturity" and "firmness" in reference to the crops. In human life stages, the Metal Phase signifies late adulthood, having to live with less mobility and potentially a decline in health.

Water

Water represents the "Greater Yin" shown by the large black area in the yin-yang symbol. Its designated color is black. As the primary source of life, water preceded all life forms on Earth. There is an interesting parallel in the Bible: "Now the earth was formless and empty, darkness was over the surface of the deep, and the Spirit of God was hovering over the waters." (Genesis 1:2) Water is associated with life, lifespan, flexibility, fluidity, calmness, wisdom, and the power to cleanse. Water is also associated with sexual energies and the reproductive system. Flexibility of Water is evident in its ability to change in form as liquid, solid, and vapor. It can also be held in containers of any shape. Water tends to flow downward, infiltrating the lowest depths—the realm ruled by yin energy.

The Water Phase

The fifth and final phase is Water. The preceding Metal Phase is the promoter of Water. The Water Phase represents the winter season where the yin energy reaches its height in the coldest of temperatures and lifeless landscape. In the human life cycle, it signifies the stage beyond late adulthood nearing death. Paradoxically, this is not far from the stage of birth or rebirth (spring). Water as energy is linked with the transcendental realm, sacredness, wisdom, and things unseen yet very much part of the human experience in life. The mystery of water is that it is formless, but it is nonetheless visible and tangible. Water lies in the liminal space between death and rebirth.

Shared Meaning of the Five Phases

The I Ching's principles are widely used in a number of Eastern disciplines from both the philosophical and the practical categories. Among the practical disciplines, the Four Pillars system, the Feng Shui system, and Oriental Medicine share the principles of the yin-yang dualism and the Five Phases, though with different emphases according to their field of research. The Four Pillars system's focus is on the dimension of time. The Feng Shui system's focus is on the dimension of space. Oriental Medicine focuses on the microcosm of the human body. Regardless of their differences, the three disciplines all highlight the practical aspects of human life. Their shared meaning of the Five Phases is organized in the following table. All of this information is used in saju interpretation.

	WOOD	FIRE	EARTH	METAL	WATER
Yin vs. Yang	yang	yang	neutral	yin	yin
Element	tree	fire	soil	metal	water
Energy	bursting	expanding	transitional	astricting	condensing
Season	spring	summer	transition	autumn	winter
Time	morning	afternoon	In-between	evening	night
Climate	wind	heat	moisture	dryness	cold
Color	green	red	yellow	white	black
Numbers	3, 8	2, 7	5, 10	4, 9	1, 6
Direction	east	south	central	west	north
Temperature	warm	hot	transitional	cool	cold
Organs	liver	heart	stomach	lungs	kidneys
Sensory	eyes	tongue	mouth	nose	ears
Taste	sour	bitter	sweet	spicy	salty
Emotion	pride	joy	thoughtful	sadness	fear
Character	kindness	civility	trust	loyalty	wisdom
Temperament	growth	passion	stubborn	composure	intuitive
Human Life-Cycle	birth to adolescence	young-adulthood	middle-age	older age	old age to death

This information reflects the general association of things, so making rigid generalizations should be avoided. A person lacking in earth energy in her saju composition, for instance, may be advised to consume foods that are sweet in nature for improving stomach health; but it would not be a prudent approach to generalize that a person with a large amount of water energy in her saju is suffering from fear. Saju charts that are composed of just one or two elements throughout the Four Pillars *can* present an analytical challenge due to the seeming imbalance of elemental energy. Such instances require sophisticated interpretation techniques and they do not always translate to a life that is out of balance.

How the Five Phases Get Along

The relationships among the Five Phases are of critical importance in the Four Pillars system. The saju charts are interpreted based on this information, so knowing them by heart is required for achieving reading proficiency. The following ten relational rules are derived from specific interactions that take place among the elements.

The Nurturers

1. Water nurtures Wood

   Trees and plants need water to live and grow. Water is the life-giving resource for Wood. Although too much water energy—e.g., destructive flooding—can be a bad thing since wood can rot in water, a healthy amount of water is essential for its well-being.

2. Wood nurtures Fire

   Fire is sustained by a continuous burning of wood. Wood is the life-giving resource for Fire. However, too much wood energy can actually extinguish the fire—imagine throwing a log onto a small fire burning on a matchstick.

3. Fire nurtures Earth

   Fire is the life-giving resource for Earth. The earth gains fertility and liveliness from the warmth provided by the sun. The frozen earth is no good for cultivating life. Too much fire energy, however, can turn the earth into a lifeless desert.

4. Earth nurtures Metal

Earth is the life-giving resource for Metal. Metallic elements are found inside the earth just as gold and diamonds are excavated from a mine. In its natural state, the metal inside the earth maintains its original form. Too much earth could suffocate the metal, preventing it from ever seeing the light outside.

5. Metal nurtures Water

Metal is the life-giving resource for Water by containing and preserving it, giving it a shape and a purpose. A metal spoon left outside overnight forms moisture on its surface as a result of condensation. Metal's cool nature and hard surface promotes Water this way. Too much metal energy is not desirable, though, since the cleansing power of water can be compromised; a cupful of water inside a very large metal basin would have difficulty staying clean.

The Controllers

1. Water controls Fire

Water controls Fire as water naturally can extinguish fire. If the fire is too big and the water too little, the fire will end up boiling the water and make it disappear in vapor. Otherwise, Fire has reasons to fear Water as its natural challenger.

2. Fire controls Metal

The cold, immobile metal can be altered in shape only when the right amount of fire energy is applied. The smelting furnace can melt metal into hot liquid that can cool down to take any shape, but this would require a significant amount of heat. Metal does not flinch in the face of any insignificant Fire, as it possesses extraordinary strength. Metal should, nevertheless, fear Fire as its natural challenger, since a small fire can still defeat a metal when given enough time to do so.

3. Metal controls Wood

   A tree is helpless before a sharp tool such as an axe that can cut it down. Metal is the natural challenger of Wood. When the tree is too big and the axe too small, the metal could break or deform. The challenger must match the energy of the challenged in order to maintain the controlling relationship.

4. Wood controls Earth

   Nothing can challenge the earth like the wood does when a tree roots itself into the soil, holding it down hard and steady. The tree's root system is also designed to absorb and take away nutrients and moisture from the soil. Wood controls Earth by controlling the soil on which it stands.

5. Earth controls Water

   Mounds of sandbags are often used to prevent flooding, as the earthen soil is the most effective element to block the flow of water. Enough amount of Earth could even close up a well or a pond. Earth is the natural challenger of Water. With too much water, however, the soil could simply wash away.

***

The ten rules are summarized in the following diagram.

The circular arrows indicate the supportive cycle where the pairs of compatible elements are standing next to each other. The arrows creating a star-like pattern start from the controller and point toward the controlled. The movement of the Five Phases revolves around the dynamics of yin and yang energies.

Interpreting with the Five Elements/Phases

It is easy to fall into the preconception that views the nurturer to be good and the controller to be bad. This may be true, as long as there is a balance to things. We must understand that too much nurturing can foster laziness, and too little control can lead to disorder and anarchy. For a balanced life, we need to be surrounded by a healthy dose of both nurturing and controlling energies.

In saju analysis, the following five cardinal rules must always be considered. The effect an element has on other elements must be explored carefully and thoroughly before arriving at an interpretative conclusion.

***

I. *Giving too much help does harm, not good.*
- Wood likes Water's nurture, but it floats on too much Water.
- Fire likes Wood's nurture, but it gets extinguished with too much Wood.
- Earth likes Fire's nurture, but it dries and cracks up with too much Fire.
- Metal likes Earth's nurture, but it suffocates with too much Earth.
- Water likes Metal's nurture, but it gets dirty with too much Metal.

II. *The helper has its limits.*
- Wood can help Fire, but too much Fire will burn Wood to ashes.

- Fire can help Earth, but too much Earth will exhaust Fire.
- Earth can help Metal, but too much Metal will enervate Earth.
- Metal can help Water, but too much Water will drown Metal.
- Water can help Wood, but too much Wood will use up Water.

III. *The controller can be harmed by the stronger counterpart.*

- Wood controls Earth, but excessive Earth can break Wood.
- Earth controls Water, but excessive Water can wash away Earth.
- Water controls Fire, but excessive Fire can dry up Water.
- Fire controls Metal, but excessive Metal can extinguish Fire.
- Metal controls Wood, but excessive Wood can deform Metal.

IV. *The weak should fear encountering the controller.*

- Weak Wood facing Metal will be cut and broken.
- Weak Fire facing Water will be extinguished.
- Weak Earth facing Wood will tilt and slide.
- Weak Metal facing Fire will melt away.
- Weak Water facing Earth will be absorbed and disappear.

V. *Excessive energy needs a nurturing task (work) in order to find balance.*

- Excessive Wood welcomes Fire, as Wood will blossom.
- Excessive Fire welcomes Earth, as Fire will be tamed.
- Excessive Earth welcomes Metal, as Earth will ease up.
- Excessive Metal welcomes Water, as Metal will mellow.
- Excessive Water welcomes Wood, as Water will slow down.

***

The rules are easy to remember as they appeal to our common senses. Applying the rules in saju analysis may not be so easy, though, since the analyst must consider and process a lot of information rather quickly and accurately in the analytical setting. Working with the Five Elements requires a careful look into the construct of the saju, including the positions of the elements, their interactions with one another, and the direction of their flow. A good directional flow starts with the Year Pillar and ends with the Hour Pillar. For instance, if Wood is found in the Year Pillar, it is favorable to find Fire in the Month Pillar as Wood naturally nurtures Fire. And it would be ideal to find Earth in the Day Pillar since Fire is the nurturer of Earth. This example represents a good directional flow, as long as Fire is not excessive so that Earth can appreciate its support.

Assessing the elemental balance in the Four Pillars is the primary task of the analyst. The quality of a saju is determined by the balance between wetness and dryness, and heat and cold. Saju compositions that are too wet, too dry, too cold, or too hot can be considered out of balance, which is translatable to the quality of life experienced by the saju owner.

Fortunately, a saju can utilize its luck cycles to find balance. (The luck cycles can also disrupt the balance in the saju.) The luck cycles that uniquely accompany a saju chart need to be evaluated in relation to the entire saju composition. When working with the luck cycles, the focus should be on how they interact with the Day Pillar—particularly the Day Master—in the saju chart.

Metaphorically, a saju is a car, and the accompanying set of luck cycles is the road that the car is traveling on. Some cars are top of the line vehicles while other cars are barely functional. Some roads are rocky and curvy while other roads are freshly paved highways. The most ideal situation would be to have a powerful car to travel on a wide and straight highway (what a life that would be!), but this cannot always be the case. We have to make the most out of life with the car and the road given to us. The secret to success in life, however, is not only dependent on the quality of the car and the road; it also depends on the individual behind the steering wheel. The will power and determination of the driver will ultimately define the journey and his or her final destination.

***

Chapter 5 Exercise

1. Explore the elements in your saju chart. Record the number of Wood, Fire, Earth, Metal, and Water. Identify any excessive or missing element.
2. Explore the elements in the saju chart(s) of your significant other(s.) Record the number of Wood, Fire, Earth, Metal, and Water. Identify any excessive or missing element.
3. Evaluate the compatibility between your saju and one other person's by comparing the elements occupying the Day Pillars. Compare the Day Stems (the Day Masters) then compare the Day Branches. Identify the elemental relationship between the Stems and the Branches in the two charts.

Chapter 6 The Ten Heavenly Stems

Look deep into nature, and you will understand everything better.
Albert Einstein

Each Pillar in a saju is made up of two characters, with one on the top and one on the bottom. The character on the top row is called the Heavenly Stem, or Stem for short. The character on the bottom row is called the Earthly Branch, or Branch for short. There are ten Heavenly Stems and twelve Earthly Branches. These constitute the alphabet of the Four Pillars system—the twenty-two Han characters in total.

The Han characters are not that difficult to learn, especially since you don't need to learn to write them, unless you want to. Unlike in the olden days, we now have digital saju calculators that instantly output a saju chart with all of its eight characters when you input the birthdate information. The saju calculators are computer-programmed TTY calendars; they are available on websites and on apps you can purchase. I sometimes reference the printed version of the TTY calendar in the book form to verify the accuracy of a chart, but I routinely use an app to construct the charts—this saves a lot of time.

There are about forty thousand Han characters (*hanzi*) that exist to this date, out of which about seven thousand are estimated to be in usage in China. This comes after the language reform in the mid-twentieth century when commonly used Han characters underwent significant simplification. In Japan, approximately eleven hundred Han characters (*kanji*) are commonly used in combination with the Japanese language. The Han characters (*hanja*) are used in Korea as well, especially in written works, but since the invention of *Hangeul*—the Korean

Alphabet—by King Sejong the Great (1397~1450), it has become possible for all written communication to take place entirely in Korean.

The twenty-two Han characters introduced in this and the next chapters mostly do not belong in the commonly used category in any context, and they are unique to the Four Pillars system. It will be helpful to think of them as symbols representing energies and elements, because underneath their complex visual design, that's what they are.

The Heavenly Stems

壬 癸

庚　　　　甲

戊 己

辛　　　　乙

丙 丁

The Ten Heavenly Stems symbolize the metaphysical realm ruled by yang energy. They represent the transcendental energies of the heavens as opposed to the earth below. On the human scale, they constitute the mind—the intellectual, psychological, and spiritual domain of existence. The Day Master and the surrounding Stems in the saju chart are thus reflective of one's thought patterns, ideas, aspirations, desires, and hopes—things that are invisible but very real and powerful in steering the life of the saju owner.

The Heavenly Stems come in the order of the Five Phases— Wood, Fire, Earth, Metal, and Water. Each Phase has its yin-yang versions so there are ten Stems in total. Since the Heavenly Stems occupy the top row and the Earthly Branches fill the bottom row in the chart, we can say that each Pillar is equipped with a Stem and a Branch, making it a Stem-Branch combination. The Stem-Branch combinations are shown vertically in the saju charts, but they can be written horizontally in other places.

1st	2nd	3rd	4th	5th	6th	7th	8th	9th	10th
yang wood	yin wood	yang fire	yin fire	yang earth	yin earth	yang metal	yin metal	yang water	yin water
甲	乙	丙	丁	戊	己	庚	辛	壬	癸
gahp	eul	byoung	jeong	moo	ghee	kyoung	shin	yim	gyeh

The first two Heavenly Stems are the yang and yin Woods. They work to nurture the next two Stems—the yang and yin Fires. The fifth and sixth Stems are the two Earths taking the center position as they are deemed "neutral." The Earths nurture the two Metals that follow. The Metals work to nurture the last two yang and yin Water Stems. The two Water Stems, in turn, nurture the Wood Stems, and the entire cycle is repeated continuously.

Out of the Ten Stems, the first five—two Woods, two Fires, and one yang Earth—are known as *yang* Stems simply because they naturally possess yang energy as elements from the yang category. The warmth of Wood, the heat of Fire, and the dryness of yang Earth are yang in character in relation to the latter Stems. The last five Stems—one yin Earth, two Metals, and two Waters—are known as *yin* Stems. The yin Stems possess yin energy in the form of moist yin Earth, cool Metal, and cold Water. The yang Stems are obviously the warm to hot group, as reflected by the color they naturally possess. They represent the spring and summer seasons. The yin Stems are the cool to cold assembly of elements, representing autumn and winter. The Ten Stems alternate the forces of yin and yang individually and in groups to keep the wheel of life moving along its path. Recognizing this distinction will be useful for saju interpretation purposes.

Each Stem comes with a unique set of attributes based on its element and yin-yang energy. Inherent characteristics of each Stem serve an important role in saju analysis, so they need to be examined thoroughly. It is easy for a beginning learner to treat the Stems simply as "yin wood," or "yang wood," without adequately understanding their differences. Imagine a giant sequoia tree versus a small field laced with English ivy. They both fall in the category of Wood, but they present two very different imageries, and the tree (yang wood) and the groundcover (yin wood) have a dissimilar effect on their environment.

The Characteristics of the Stems

甲 (*gahp*) is the first of the Ten Heavenly Stems. It is referred to as "Gahp Wood." The Han character resembles a fully grown tree, boasting its yang wood energy. It is a byproduct of Water and Fire. As the symbol of spring, 甲 Gahp Wood represents life in all of its vigor and vitality. It welcomes and longs for the company of 丙 (*byoung*) Fire that symbolizes the sun, just as trees need sunlight to grow and thrive. By the same token, it appreciates the company of 壬 (*yim*) Water as trees also need water. 甲 Gahp Wood is associated with bursting energy, active growth and expansion, as long as there is no metal energy to deter it.

On the psychological level, 甲 Gahp Wood embodies confidence and unwavering sense of purpose. It enjoys leadership and harbors competitive spirit. It craves for the recognition of others. As a mature tree, it is wise, generous, giving, nurturing, and teachable, often excelling in education. Many educators and thinkers tend to find 甲 Gahp Wood in their saju. 甲 Gahp Wood's weaknesses include inability to attend to details, not finishing what it started, inflexibility from overconfidence, rigidity, and sensitivity to criticism. In the face of life's challenges (e.g., illnesses, accidents, relationship issues, etc.), 甲 Gahp Wood has the capacity to overcome minor setbacks, but when it falls, it can fall hard.

Order of Strokes:

甲 甲 甲 甲 甲

Symbols: trees, pillars, thunder

Meaning: leadership, beginning, planning, honor, pride, competition, straight, self-esteem, confidence, stubbornness, loneliness

Harmonious Combination: 甲 and 己 (Gahp Wood + Ghee Earth)

Clashing Opposition: 甲 vs. 庚 (Gahp Wood vs. Kyoung Metal)

乙 (*eul*) is the second Heavenly Stem in order. It is referred to as "Eul Wood," the yin version of the Wood Phase. The Han character resembles a sprouting nascent herb. Edible vegetation and crops fall into the category of 乙 Eul Wood and its yin wood energy.

Characteristically, 乙 Eul Wood carries the hallmark of practicality. It is tenacious and flexible, bursting through the dense earth to sprout and adjusting to its environment for survival and growth. Flowers, weeds, vines, and groundcovers are examples of 乙 Eul Wood's tendency to subsist in the yin realm close to the earth. 乙 Eul Woods may be less noticeable and appear vulnerable, but they are full of life energy, determination, stubbornness, and are quite independent.

People with 乙 Eul Woods in their prime Pillars often have delicate, attractive facial features. They can easily stand out in beauty and charm others with their fashion sensibility. Independent 乙 Eul Woods are less likely to reach out to others for help, and they prefer to do things on their own, which can make them become prone to feeling lonely. They are successful with tasks that require patience, endurance, and determination once they accept the level of practicality in the task.

Order of Strokes:

Symbols: herbs, plants, flowers, ground covers, wind

Meaning: patience, stubbornness, curvature, fashionista, delicate, introvert, sensitive, attractive, service

Harmonious Combination: 乙 and 庚 (Eul Wood + Kyoung Metal)

Clashing Opposition: 乙 vs. 辛 (Eul Wood vs. Shin Metal)

丙 (byoung) is the third Heavenly Stem. It is referred to as "Byoung Fire." It is known to symbolize the sun. As yang fire, it boasts tremendous energy that translates into vitality, activity, movement on large scale, transformation, expressiveness, extremity, resistance to injustice, extroversion, competition, and excitable temperament. 丙 Byoung Fire seeks to influence and change the world with its radiating presence. Its mission is to selflessly, in good faith, help others. It is associated with dispersing energy, ambition, and high self-esteem as sunlight is needed and wanted by all.

People with 丙 Byoung Fire in their saju are well mannered, fluent in speech, passionate, entertaining, and they also tend to have an attractive appearance. They easily attract the attention of other people. The glamorous 丙 Byoung Fire Day Masters are never without drama—in both good and not so good ways—in their lives. Many entertainers have 丙 Byoung Fire in their prime Pillars—the Month, Day, or Hour Pillar. As the Fire from the heavenly realm, 丙 Byoung Fire is not exactly the type of fire energy to reshape Metal (as sunlight cannot melt metal on its own), and is hence lacking in practicality.

Order of Strokes:

Symbols: sun, light

Meaning: bright, glamor, extravagant, outgoing, relationship, language, courtesy, civility, assertive, culture, openness, proud, arrogance, service

Harmonious Combination: 丙 and 辛 (Byoung Fire + Shin Metal)

Clashing Opposition: 丙 vs. 壬 (Byoung Fire vs. Yim Water)

丁 (*jeong*) is the fourth Heavenly Stem. It is referred to as "Jeong Fire," the yin version of the Fire Phase. 丁 Jeong Fire represents small things that give off subtle light or heat, including starlight, moonlight, lamplight, candlelight, flashlight, camp fire, etc. Symbolizing Fire from the earthly realm, 丁 Jeong Fires are practical, providing heat and light where it is needed.

丁 Jeong Fires are warm, bright, affectionate, humane, kind, friendly, and sacrificial. 丁 Jeong Fire Day Masters can easily suffer a loss because of their selfless, blind attitude in helping others. They need dry Wood nearby to burn continuously and to achieve their purpose. They also like to see 庚 Kyoung Metal nearby, which gives them work to do, since they can melt and shape metal. Giving off subtle light and heat suitable for lighting and warming up dark places, 丁 Jeong Fires are good at finding things and making discoveries that require careful attention to details. People with 丁 Jeong Fire in their sajus make good helpers such as counselors, researchers, analysts, investigators and educators.

Order of Strokes:

Symbols: candle light, lamp light, camp fire, lighthouse, moonlight, star

Meaning: warmth, cheerful, humane, expressive, kind hearted, civilization, service, thoughtful, sacrificial, relationship

Harmonious Combination: 丁 and 壬 (Jeong Fire + Yim Water)

Clashing Opposition: 丁 vs. 癸 (Jeong Fire vs. Gyeh Water)

戊 (*moo*) is the fifth Heavenly Stem. It is referred to as "Moo Earth." Energy wise, it is a yang earth, representing large land

masses such as a great, sprawling mountain. The Han character resembles a cross-legged person resting on a rock, drinking water after a big hike. Another name for 戊 Moo Earth is "High Mountain-Dry Earth," given its enormous size and energy. It serves as a gigantic repository of natural resources, supporting all life forms including forests, animals, birds, insects, etc.

戊 Moo Earths are tolerant, and they tend to embrace the outside world rather than reveal their inner world. Trust is an important virtue to them, and they would rather associate with a small group of people they can trust. They often exhibit high self-esteem and strong leadership. 戊 Moo Earth Day Master bosses can be difficult since they are less likely to change or compromise. 戊 Moo Earths are associated with transitional energy, motherly instinct, leadership, tolerance, and immobility that can translate into a kind of stubbornness others find difficult to relate to.

Order of Strokes:

Symbols: mountain, hill, dam, earthen soil

Meaning: central, neutrality, broad shaped, overweight, drive, grit, stubbornness, trust, storage, quiet, parsimony, Mother Earth

Harmonious Combination: 戊 and 癸 (Moo Earth + Gyeh Water)

Controlling Relationship: 戊 vs. 甲 (Moo Earth is controlled by Gahp Wood)

己 (*ghee*) is the sixth Heavenly Stem. It is referred to as "Ghee Earth," the yin version of the Earth Phase. 己 Ghee Earth represents small, cultivable lands such as farmlands and gardens. The Han character resembles an outline of a parceled land. Another name for 己 Ghee Earth is "Domestic Field-Moist Earth." Similar to 戊 Moo Earth, 己 Ghee Earth excels in leading, mothering, and helping others, but it is more proactive, intentional, and practical in doing so. Its connection to the domestic habitat generates a sense of stability that can translate into a kind of passive nature. Not having the expansive perspective as 戊 Moo Earth does, small-mindedness is an attribute of 己 Ghee Earth.

己 Ghee Earth Day Masters prefer to keep things to themselves and are less likely to open up. They are conservative in temperament but sociable, and tend to maintain relationships well by tolerating and embracing others. Given their highly developed practical nature, 己 Ghee Earths can be viewed as opportunists, and they are talented in making connections with people. A 己 Ghee Earth does not like to see a 壬 Yim Water nearby, since the two will not only create muddy water together, but 己 Ghee Earth's identity and purpose would be lost in the process.

Order of Strokes:

Symbols: cultivated field, parcel, low landscape, dirt

Meaning: mediator, conservative, self-care, center, dust, roads, sincere, practical

Harmonious Combination: 己 and 甲 (Ghee Earth + Gahp Wood)

Controlling Relationship: 己 vs. 乙 (Ghee Earth is controlled by Eul Wood)

庚 (*kyoung*) is the seventh Heavenly Stem. It is referred to as "Kyoung Metal." As a yang metal, it represents large-sized metals such as steels and machineries used in heavy industries. In its natural state, it represents large rocks and boulders. 庚 Kyoung Metal is the most firm, dense, and impenetrable

Heavenly Stem. It projects an air of strength, pride, and, sometimes, aggression. It is one of the more powerful Stems given its toughness as an element.

庚 Kyoung Metal Day Masters have strong personalities. They are strong willed, uncompromising, and they seek the attention of others through self-display. Then can be intense and even explosive when placed under heavy pressure. (The strong tends to break under pressure when the weak can simply bend with flexibility.) As untamed metal, 庚 Kyoung Metal longs for the heat energy of 丁 Jeong Fire that can shape it into something useful. It also appreciates the company of 壬 Yim Water that can keep it clean and calmed.

Order of Strokes:

Symbols: boulder, steel, metal weapons (sword, ax, etc.), machinery, vehicles, industrial heavy equipment

Meaning: perfection, loyal, dignity, belligerence, revolution, strength, hard, stubborn, ideal, unable to compromise

Harmonious Combination: 庚 and乙 (Kyoung Metal + Eul Wood)

Clashing Opposition: 庚 vs. 甲 (Kyoung Metal vs. Gahp Wood)

辛 (*shin*) is the eighth Heavenly Stem. It is referred to as "Shin Metal," the yin version of the Metal Phase. 辛 Shin Metal represents sharp objects such as knives, needles, and hand-held metal tools and weapons already tamed by fire. Clouds, frost, precious stones and metals that shimmer also make the list.

辛 Shin Metal possesses exceptional firmness and sharpness characterized by utility and ferocity. It prefers 丙 Byoung Fire (sunlight) over 丁 Jeong Fire (heat) that can make it shine; it doesn't need any more heat. It longs for the company of 壬 Yim Water to stay clean and sparkly. 辛 Shin Metal is associated with astricting energy, spiciness, brilliance, severity, loneliness, and innovation. 辛 Shin Metal Day Masters are sensitive, fastidious, considerate, responsible, and they hold high self-esteem that can come across as being arrogant.

Order of Strokes:

64

Symbols: knife, needle, drill, bullet, precious stones, jewelry

Meaning: perfectionist, sharp, sensitive, ferocity, civility, pride, suffering, separation, cloud, frost

Harmonious Combination: 辛 and 丙 (Shin Metal + Byoung Fire)

Clashing Opposition: 辛 vs. 乙 (Shin Metal vs. Eul Wood)

壬 (yim) is the ninth Heavenly Stem. It is referred to as "Yim Water." As a yang water, it represents large bodies of water such as oceans and sizable lakes. 壬 Yim Water is quite mobile and flexible, and it possesses a sense of openness beyond ordinary trends. It wields enormous strength and influence, affecting both the earth and the atmosphere in vapor, fluid, or solid forms. In cold environments, 壬 Yim Water's mobility decreases.

People with 壬 Yim Water in their prime Pillars can attract attention and exude charisma. Wisdom, courtesy, courage, adaptability, and decisiveness are aspects of their character. As the basic source of life, the water element naturally possesses nurturing energy. In its stillness, 壬 Yim Water's depth is unfathomable, which makes 壬 Yim Water Day Masters quiet people who are not quick to share what's on their mind. Though 壬 Yim Waters prefer calmness and can be quite patient, they can be volatile without reservation, just as a powerful tsunami can sweep away everything in its path.

Order of Strokes:

Symbols: water, lake, river water, ocean

Meaning: flexible, decisive, wise, uncontrollable, storm, communication, darkness, depth, mystery, volatility

Harmonious Combination: 壬 and 丁 (Yim Water + Jeong Fire)

Clashing Opposition: 壬 vs. 丙 (Yim Water vs. Byoung Fire)

癸 (gyeh) is the tenth and final Heavenly Stem. It is referred to as "Gyeh Water," the yin version of the Water Phase. It represents small streams, rain, fog, and small bodies of water such as a pond. 癸 Gyeh Water is different from 壬 Yim Water in that it supports life on the human scale. It is readily consumable, being practical and self-sacrificial. 癸 Gyeh Water must flow continuously in order to sustain its vitality (e.g., bloodstreams, faucet water, etc.), otherwise it could rot and attract filth. As a practical water form, it can consolidate and solidify things with its power of cohesion—as in adding water to flour to make a dough. 癸 Gyeh Water is associated with the life energy in the human body, including the reproductive system, and it supports and organizes the natural environment for birth (and rebirth) in the upcoming season of 甲 Gahp Wood (spring).

The yin energy of water is heightened in 癸 Gyeh Water, so 癸 Gyeh Water Day Masters often have a yin personality as introverts. At the same time, they have active imaginations and are quite sensitive, humane, and humble. They long for the presence of 丙 Byoung Fire in the need for yang energy for balance.

Order of Strokes:

Symbols: rain water, small stream, snow, dew, water drops

Meaning: perseverance, sensitive, information, smart, frost, separation, solitude, spiritual

Harmonious Combination: 癸 and 戊 (Gyeh Water + Moo Earth)

Clashing Opposition: 癸 vs. 丁 (Gyeh Water vs. Jeong Fire)

Chapter 6 Exercise

1. Explore the four Stems in your saju chart. Which Stems appear in your Year, Month, Day, and Hour Pillars? The Day Stem represents you, so go ahead and review its characteristics.

2. Explore the Stems in the saju chart(s) of your significant other(s).

Chapter 7 The Twelve Earthly Branches

The earth is the very quintessence of the human condition.
Hannah Arendt

The Earthly Branches are representative of the earthly realm ruled by yin energy. They symbolize the things on the earth that can be seen, touched, and experienced in concrete terms. They involve the vicissitudes of the mundane world and have a visible effect on human surroundings and circumstances. The Earthly Branches are the generators of *"shin-sahl,"* a term that translates to "gods and curses"; and this is what makes them a more complex bunch than the Heavenly Stems. Imagine flying an airplane in the sky versus driving a car on a busy road. The plane has almost zero probability of bumping into another plane, but the car on the ground has to navigate with vigilance to make sure it doesn't hit anything on its path to destination. The destiny of the Branches is like that of the car.

The Earthly Branches come in the order of Water, Wood, Fire, Metal, and back to Water—in the sequence of the four seasons of the year. (This order is in line with each year starting with winter in January and ending with winter in December.) There are twelve Earthly Branches which is two more than the Heavenly Stems. This is because there are *four* Earth Phase Earthly Branches serving as the transitional links between the seasons. All other Phases—Wood, Fire, Metal, and Water—come in pairs of their yin-yang versions.

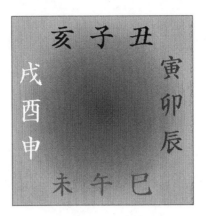

The need for four Earth Phase Branches reveals an important aspect of the nature of the Branches. Because the Branches represent objects and phenomena from the physical world, the transformation of energy is a slower process. In other words, it takes more time for the Branches to transition from one form of energy (or phase) to the next. For instance, when a heater is turned on inside a room, the air in the room can warm up quickly, but a table or a sofa in the room will take much longer to warm up to match the temperature of the heated air. This example sums up the difference between the Stems and the Branches, or the difference between energy and matter: The metaphysical energy of the Stems transitions faster in relation to the physical energy of the Branches that requires more time to transition—hence the four Earth Phase Branches that fill the transitional periods.

Unlike the Heavenly Stems, the Earthly Branches are endowed with a set of animal symbols. The Twelve Branches come in the order of Rat, Ox, Tiger, Rabbit, Dragon, Snake, Horse, Sheep, Monkey, Rooster, Dog, and Pig. The animals are representative of the earthly realm as they can be found in close proximity to human life, except for the dragon which is a mythical, imaginary creature.

No one knows the exact basis for the connection between the animals and the Earthly Branches, but there is one theory that suggests that the number of the animals' toenails had determined their order and their yin-yang energy. Since odd numbers are yang in energy and even numbers are yin, the number of toenails would have placed the animals in either the yin or the yang category. The snake, having no feet, is given the yin status due to its tongue that splits into two.

The Earthly Branch sequence begins and ends with the Water Phase, which is equivalent to the winter season. Emphasis on the water element is an affirmation of Water's association with death and rebirth, the end and the beginning of life.

1st	2nd	3rd	4th	5th	6th	7th	8th	9th	10th	11th	12th
yang water	yin earth	yang wood	yin wood	yang earth	yin fire	yang fire	yin earth	yang metal	yin metal	yang earth	yin water
子	丑	寅	卯	辰	巳	午	未	申	酉	戌	亥
jah	chook	inn	myo	jin	sah	oh	mee	shin	yoo	sool	hae

The Characteristics of the Branches

子 (*jah*) is the first Earthly Branch. It is referred to as "Jah Water." Yang in energy, 子 Jah Water symbolizes fertility and reproduction as life begins and abounds in water. The highly fertile rat is placed here for this reason. Just as rats are active in the darkness of the night, the dark, cold wintry season is when the yin energy reaches its height in the form of 子 Jah Water.

The Han character 子 Jah is commonly used to refer to a "son" or an "offspring," but in the Four Pillars system, it is read as 子 Jah Water with the animal symbol of Rat. Character wise, 子 Jah Water presents well-developed instinct, intelligence, and sensibility. In the depth of its cool, clear water, 子 Jah Water harbors an air of secrecy. 子 Jah Day Branches are associated with wealth, dignity, diligence, kindness, attractiveness, yet they tend to be passive in attitude and a bit egotistic. They love to eat late night meals.

Midnight, or the 子 Jah Water Hour proper, is known as the hour of heaven's opening, and rituals for honoring the deceased ancestors are traditionally held at this hour in some Asian cultures. 子 Jah Water Hour (23:00 ~ 00:59) represents the first hour of the day.

Order of Strokes:

Symbols: rat, offspring, seed, tears

Meaning: cold winter, dark night, water, fertility, reproduction, (sexual) stamina, black, mystery, transcendental realm, liminal space, ears, kidney

Harmonious Combinations: 子丑 (water earth) / 亥子丑 (water) / 申子辰 (water)

Clashing Opposition: 子 vs. 午 (Jah Water vs. Oh Fire)

丑 (*chook*) is the second Earthly Branch. It is referred to as "Chook Earth." It comes in yin energy. 丑Chook Earth takes charge of the transition period from winter to spring, marking the end of winter. As a slowly thawing wintry earth, 丑 Chook Earth is still cold, hard, and wet. It is known as the *Storage of Metal*—the previous (autumn) season's lingering energy. The stored-up (or locked-up) metal energy deep inside the丑 Chook Earth is now unable to hinder the coming of the next season of spring along with its wood energy. 丑 Chook Earth has the capacity to mutate into either Water or Metal depending on the set of Branches it merges with.

The animal ox is associated with being industrious and patient. Oxen were invaluable animals for agriculture throughout history, and in their lack of activity during the cold winter months, they patiently wait for the arrival of spring. 丑 Chook Earth boasts endurance and diligence (especially in repetitive tasks and physical labor), but it can exhibit stubbornness and impetuousness that can lead to interpersonal conflict.

丑 Chook Earth Day Branches are believed to possess karmic energy originating from the saju owner's previous life; and they may be prone to experiencing a tumultuous life with notable health and relationship issues. Engaging in spiritual practice (e.g., meditation, prayer) and building up good karma through good deeds and good intent can help alleviate the challenges they may have to face.

Order of Strokes:

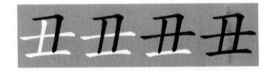

Symbols: ox, frozen soil, wet earth, cultivated land

Meaning: Storage of Metal, endurance, patience, hardworking, overwork, suffering, secret, stubbornness

Harmonious Combinations: 子丑 (water earth) / 亥子丑 (water) / 巳酉丑 (metal)

Clashing Opposition: 丑 vs. 未 (Chook Earth vs. Mee Earth)

寅 (*inn*) is the third Earthly Branch. It is referred to as "Inn Wood." Yang in energy, 寅 Inn Wood possesses tremendous force as the symbol of a new beginning. The Lunar New Year begins with the month of Tiger. Tiger symbolizes strength, fearlessness, courage, dignity, honor, and speed. The image of the tiger is often used in talismans for protection and keeping the evil spirits away.

As the birthplace of Fire, 寅 Inn Wood exudes warmth, growth, and hopeful prospects in the glory of the spring season. It works hard to create the perfect environment for the arrival of the Fire Phase (summer). Photosynthesis is an important function of a tree; and it is largely responsible for maintaining oxygen in Earth's atmosphere, and fire needs oxygen to burn. The creative process of photosynthesis also supplies the energy necessary for life on Earth, attesting to the nurturing energy of Wood as an element.

The independent, aspirational 寅 Inn Woods excel in leadership with unmatched driving force for success. They would rather be a boss than a follower. The 寅 Inn Wood Day Branches can appear self-righteous and dogmatic, but their inward nature is warm and giving. Exercising humility is good for maintaining harmonious interpersonal relationships.

Order of Strokes:

Symbols: tiger, tree, log, early morning

Meaning: beginning, spring, courage, strength, sacred spirit, departure, travel (via ground), transportation, education, culture, east

Harmonious Combinations: 寅亥 (wood) / 寅卯辰 (wood) / 寅午戌 (fire)

Clashing Opposition: 寅 vs. 申 (Inn Wood vs. Shin Metal)

卯 (*myo*) is the fourth Earthly Branch. It is referred to as "Myo Wood." Though yin in energy, 卯 Myo Wood is known as the king of Wood Phase, as the wood energy reaches its height during the 卯 Myo Wood month. It may lack the forceful, bursting energy of 寅 Inn Wood, but 卯 Myo Wood is considered to be the mature version, being better established on the soil and having dominated its environment.

The Han character resembles a pair of rabbit's ears. With their big, long ears, rabbits are sensitive to hearing, an important sense for survival. People with 卯 Myo Woods possess sensitive, analytical personalities and delicate taste. They are sensitive to change in their surroundings and are quick to adapt. They tend to be strong-willed realists, while drawn to pursue spirituality and faith practices. 卯 Myo Woods are vulnerable against metal energy (especially yin metal) that can hurt them, so it is best to take precautions.

Order of Strokes:

Symbols: rabbit, flower, plant, bine, herbs

Meaning: delicate, sensitive, news, artistic, painting, fashion, change, attractiveness

Harmonious Combinations: 卯戌 (fire) / 寅卯辰 (wood) / 亥卯未 (wood)

Clashing Opposition: 卯 vs. 酉 (Myo Wood vs. Yoo Metal)

辰 (*jin*) is the fifth Earthly Branch. It is referred to as "Jin Earth." Yang in energy, 辰 Jin Earth marks the end of spring and transitions toward summer. It is the *Storage of Water*, the previous (winter) season's lingering energy. The stored-up water energy stays inactive for the arrival of the next season, where the fire energy continues to increase during the summer months. The 辰 Jin Earth month (April) is a time of earthly movements caused by thawing and warming of the soil, causing strong winds (tornadoes) and trembling earth (earthquakes).

The dragon is the only mythical animal among the twelve animals, and it frequently appears in Eastern legendary tales involving fantastical narratives. The eye-catching imagery continues to appear today in festive celebrations as the symbol of power and greatness. The mysterious and domineering image of the dragon is reflected in 辰 Jin Earth's characteristics. 辰 Jin

Earth Day Branches are high achievers with strong personalities and they have the ability to attract wealth. They can be movers and shakers with their intelligence, skill sets and strategy. But as a wet and woody Earth that is in transition, the inner world of 辰 Jin Earth is more complex. 辰 Jin Earths can be arrogant and too proud to accept or appreciate others. They are quick to change their minds, which is in line with 辰 Jin Earth's mutative nature. As a neutral Earth, 辰 Jin Earth can side with either Wood or Water depending on the set of Branches it merges with.

Order of Strokes:

Symbols: dragon, wet earth, golden earth, cultivated soil

Meaning: Storage of Water, divinity, power, design, drastic change, balance, hidden, adaptive, reproductive organs, stomach, wealth

Harmonious Combinations: 辰酉 (metal) / 寅卯辰 (wood) / 申子辰 (water)

Clashing Opposition: 辰 vs. 戌 (Jin Earth vs. Sool Earth)

巳 (*sah*) is the sixth Earthly Branch. It is referred to as "Sah Fire." 巳 Sah Fire commands the beginning of summer. Though yin in energy, 巳 Sah Fire is used as yang fire in saju interpretation. (The reason for this is explained in Chapter 11.) 巳 Sah Fire is the birthplace of Metal, as it begins to pave the way for the upcoming season of Metal (autumn). Hence, it has the ability to mutate into metal energy depending on the set of Branches it merges with.

The Han character 巳 resembles a snake, an animal that hibernates during the cold months and thrives in a sultry environment. (巳 Sah Fire should not be confused with the Stem, 己 Ghee Earth, as they share a visual resemblance.) 巳 Sah Fire is characterized by independence, movement and civility. It is intuitive, wise and insightful; even the scripture urges us to be "wise as a serpent." It can also be furiously explosive, just as a poisonous snake can launch a fearsome attack when it needs to.

巳 Sah Fire is associated with travel luck, particularly by plane. People with 巳 Sah Fire in their prime Pillars do well in careers involving travel and they make a resonating impact wherever they go. The downside to this is instability and a lack of security.

Order of Strokes:

Symbols: snake, sun, airplane

Meaning: change, travel (via plane), flamboyance, poison, competitiveness, tenacity, crossroads, culture, education, theater

Harmonious Combinations: 巳申 (water) / 巳午未 (fire) / 巳酉丑 (metal)

Clashing Opposition: 巳 vs. 亥 (Sah Fire vs. Hae Water)

午 (*oh*) is the seventh Earthly Branch. It is referred to as "Oh Fire." 午 Oh Fire represents the peak of the Fire Phase, the middle of hot summer. The wild and passionate horse is used to depict this season. Though yang in energy, 午 Oh Fire is used as yin Fire in saju interpretation. (The reason for this is explained in Chapter 11.) 午 Oh Fire stands at the opposite pole from 子 Jah Water, and twelve noon is the 午 Oh Fire Hour proper (11:00 ~ 12:59).

Horses are sensitive animals and don't cope well with drastic changes. But they are also resilient, and they portray a burning flame when they gallop. 午 Oh Fires are associated with advancement of civilization, wealth, divine blessings, fame, and civility. Fire (flame) is vulnerable to gusting winds which can translate into a type of identity crisis under unfavorable circumstances. 午 Oh Fire Day Branches are active, energetic, and have strong personalities. Excessive fire energy in the saju can lead to impatience, talkativeness, excitable temperament, inability to focus, or impulsivity.

Order of Strokes:

Symbols: horse, fire, light

Meaning: noon, passionate, herd, eyesight, stamina, intellectual culture, extremity

Harmonious Combination: 午未 (fire earth) / 巳午未 (fire) / 寅午戌 (fire)

Clashing Opposition: 午 vs. 子 (Oh Fire vs. Jah Water)

未 (*mee*) is the eighth Earthly Branch. It is referred to as "Mee Earth." Yin in energy, 未 Mee Earth marks the transition from summer to autumn. It is a hot, dry earth in charge of processing the accumulated heat energy from the months of 巳 Sah and 午

Oh Fires. 未 Mee Earth is the *Storage of Wood*, the lingering wood energy from the previous season of spring. The wood energy is stored up so that it doesn't clash with the metal energy of the next season of autumn. This makes 未 Mee Earth the deathbed of wood energy, as all growth halts while ripening continues to progress during this period.

The animal sheep is associated with gentleness and docility, and a kind of stubbornness domesticated animals can display. They love to roam around the land, even near the hazardous cliffs. The 未 Mee Earth Day Branches do better mentally and physically when they are able to travel periodically rather than staying put in one place for extended periods of time. They are committed to accumulating wealth and tend to stay busy in doing so. They prefer a quiet living environment as opposed to a bustling city life.

Order of Strokes:

Symbols: sheep, hot and dry earth, wild land

Meaning: Storage of Wood, sheepish, taste, stubbornness, temper

Harmonious Combinations: 午未 (fire earth) / 巳午未 (fire) / 亥卯未 (wood)

Clashing Opposition: 未 vs. 丑 (Mee Earth vs. Chook Earth)

申 (shin*) is the ninth Earthly Branch. It is referred to as "Shin Metal." It is yang in energy. The 申 Shin Metal month marks the beginning of autumn as the temperatures begin to drop in the atmosphere. This Branch is symbolized by Monkey, the animal that resembles humans the most out of the twelve. Monkeys are clever and nimble-fingered, and with their appetite for food, they are speedy eaters. They display humane qualities with their expressions of human feelings.

申 Shin Metal is associated with talent, purity, sentimentality, decency, loneliness, money and travel. The 申 Shin Metal Day Branches are prone to experiencing aloneness regardless of their relationship status, thus consciously and proactively managing depressive moods may prevent future problems. An alternative approach to dealing with an internal sense of solitude would be to profess religious practices or to travel periodically. They tend to be gentle people, equipped with a resounding voice (like a gong), and they like to stay busy with work. 申 Shin Metals appreciate the presence of Water nearby that can keep them clean and active.

*申 Shin Metal (a yang Branch) should not be confused with 辛 Shin Metal (a yin Stem) as they share the same name and element.

Order of Strokes:

Symbols: monkey, steel, metallic products

Meaning: talent, nimble-fingered, travel, money, smart, adaptive, greed, soul, autumn, harvest, lonesomeness, self-centeredness

Harmonious Combinations: 申巳 (water) / 申酉戌 (metal) / 申子辰 (water)

Clashing Opposition: 申 vs. 寅 (Shin Metal vs. Inn Wood)

酉 (yoo) is the tenth Earthly Branch. It is referred to as "Yoo Metal." Yin in energy, 酉 Yoo Metal is the toughest element among the Branches. It is the king of Metal, as metal energy reaches its height in 酉 Yoo Metal. Roosters crow at the break of dawn—the morning hours of the Wood Phase. Thus, 酉 Yoo Metal poses as the mortal adversary of 卯 Myo Wood, the king of Wood Phase. In traditional weddings, live roosters were part of the ceremony as a symbol for a new beginning. Roosters were also used in religious rituals as sacrifices in light of the extraordinary spiritual energy they are believed to possess.

酉 Yoo Metals are intuitive, spiritual, and decisive, and they can be self-absorbed with their own feelings and thoughts. They come with strong personalities marked by sensitivity, charisma, and stubbornness. They are drawn to careers that deal with sharp objects such as knives, needles, and other metallic tools and devices. Surgeons, doctors, lapidaries, and locksmiths make the list. The 酉 Yoo Metal Day Branches tend to have high self-esteem and assurance of self-identity. They know what they want, and are likely to attempt to correct others because they are set in their own ways.

Order of Strokes:

Symbols: rooster, jewelry, currency, bell, needle, mirror, spices

Meaning: newness, art of medicine, white, frost, sensitive, skin, teeth, lungs, cloud, bell sound, cleanliness

Harmonious Combinations: 酉辰 (metal) 申酉戌 (metal) / 巳酉丑 (metal)

Clashing Opposition: 酉 vs. 卯 (Yoo Metal vs. Myo Wood)

戌 (*sool*) is the eleventh Earthly Branch. It is referred to as "Sool Earth." Yang in energy, 戌 Sool Earth is in charge of the transition period from autumn to winter. The imagery of shriveled up fall leaves rolling on a dusty ground informs that 戌 Sool Earth is a dry, arid earth. It is the *Storage of Fire*, the lingering fire energy from the previous season of summer. The stored-up fire energy stays inactive for the arrival of the next season of winter and its water energy. The Han character is almost identical to the fifth Heavenly Stem, 戊 Moo Earth, except for the extra dot on the left.

The animal dog is associated with loyalty, wisdom, shrewdness, stubbornness, and religiosity. 戌 Sool Earths are deep thinkers who are attracted to the metaphysical world; they are drawn to spirituality, art, religion, and philosophy. As an earth element with the capacity to store, 戌 Sool Earths are able to accumulate wealth, unless they are heavy spenders. If they can't resist the temptation to spend, investing in real estate can be an option to protect their wealth. 戌 Sool Earth Day Branches possess artistic and analytical talents with interest in literature and epicurean lifestyle. Practicing religious faith and philanthropy can empower their chosen way of life.

Order of Strokes:

Symbols: dog, earthen soil, spear, sword

Meaning: Storage of Fire, loyalty, fighter, smart, vigilant, religion, prayer

Harmonious Combinations: 戌卯 (fire) / 申酉戌 (metal) / 寅午戌 (fire)

Clashing Opposition: 戌 vs. 辰 (Sool Earth vs. Jin Earth)

亥 (*hae*) is the twelfth and last Earthly Branch. It is referred to as "Hae Water." 亥 Hae Water marks the beginning of winter. Though yin in energy, it is used as yang Water in saju interpretation. (This change makes 子 Jah Water, the first Earthly Branch, a yin Water in saju interpretation.)

亥 Hae Water's clarity and depth is symbolic of a new beginning. As a flowing water, it doesn't look back but moves forward, with adaptability to change. 亥 Hae Waters value freedom, and they may show a lack of patience or endurance when their freedom is compromised. They tend to overthink, which may result in a depressive mood. 亥 Hae Waters are bright, sensible, friendly, and intuitive. They are also known for their resounding voice.

The 亥 Hae Water Day Branches can easily sacrifice themselves over other people to the point of being regretful. So, cultivating self-awareness and not making hasty decisions are encouraged. If there is a 戌 Sool Earth nearby, the 戌亥 Sool-Hae combination (called "Heaven's Gate Star") will surely open up one's mind to explore the world of metaphysics and spirituality.

Order of Strokes:

Symbols: pig, lake, river, pond

Meaning: night, overweight, omnivorous, tree, greed, faith, service, travel, movement, intuition, language, spirituality

Harmonious Combinations: 亥寅 (wood) / 亥子丑 (water) / 亥卯未 (wood)

Clashing Opposition: 亥 vs. 巳 (Hae Water vs. Sah Fire)

The Earthly Branches and the Twelve Months

The Twelve Earthly Branches are closely associated with the twelve months of the year, each Branch representing a period of one month. Traditionally, these are lunar calendar months that can be translated into the solar (Gregorian) calendar months. The first (lunar) month of the year is represented by 寅 Inn Wood, the third Branch in order, and this particular month falls on February in the solar calendar. The 寅 Inn Wood marks the beginning of spring; hence the lunar calendar year always begins with the season of spring.

The following table lists both the lunar and the solar months and the animal symbols associated with the months. The demarcations between the months do not overlap exactly between the solar and the lunar dates, so this is presented in approximation.

Earthly Branch		Lunar Month	Solar Month
寅	Inn Wood	Month of Tiger	February
卯	Myo Wood	Month of Rabbit	March
辰	Jin Earth	Month of Dragon	April
巳	Sah Fire	Month of Snake	May
午	Oh Fire	Month of Horse	June
未	Mee Earth	Month of Sheep	July
申	Shin Metal	Month of Monkey	August
酉	Yoo Metal	Month of Rooster	September
戌	Sool Earth	Month of Dog	October
亥	Hae Water	Month of Pig	November
子	Jah Water	Month of Rat	December
丑	Chook Earth	Month of Ox	January

The difference between the lunar and the solar calendars is plain and simple. The solar calendar is determined by the time it takes the earth to orbit the sun divided by twelve. The earth's revolution around the sun takes about 365.25 days, and when divided into 12 months, each month is about 30.4 days long. To offset the difference between the 365-day calendar year and the actual time of revolution (365.25 days), an intercalary day is added every 4 years: February gets 29 days in the leap year instead of the usual 28 days.

The lunar calendar, on the other hand, is determined by the time it takes the moon to orbit the earth. Based on the phases of the moon, it takes about 29.5 days for one revolution to take place which is considered one month. On the lunar calendar, a month is 29 or 30 days long. This calculation, obviously, creates a significantly different timeline compared to the solar calendar, as there can only be 354 days in a lunar year. That's a difference of 11 days. After a few years, the difference can add up, and this is why the lunar calendar is equipped with a *leap month* every

2.5 years or so. The leap month helps the lunar calendar to catch up with the solar calendar. The leap month is simply squeezed into a year as the thirteenth month, but the exact placement of the leap month varies.

***

♦ When using an online saju calculator to pull up a saju chart, it is best to use the birthdate information from the solar calendar, so you don't have to be concerned with the leap months of the lunar calendar. Any lunar date can be converted to a solar date and vice versa.

The Earthly Branches and the Hours of the Day

The Twelve Earthly Branches are associated with the twelve segments of a day, with each Branch representing a period of 2 hours. The 子 Jah Water Hour is the first hour of the day, specified by the time between 23:00 and 00:59. Midnight is at the center of 子 Jah Water Hour. The Hour Pillar in the saju chart is constructed based on this information.

Earthly Branch		Hours of the Day	Time
子	Jah Water	Hour of Rat	23:00 ~ 00:59
丑	Chook Earth	Hour of Ox	01:00 ~ 02:59
寅	Inn Wood	Hour of Tiger	03:00 ~ 04:59
卯	Myo Wood	Hour of Rabbit	05:00 ~ 06:59
辰	Jin Earth	Hour of Dragon	07:00 ~ 08:59
巳	Sah Fire	Hour of Snake	09:00 ~ 10:59
午	Oh Fire	Hour of Horse	11:00 ~ 12:59
未	Mee Earth	Hour of Sheep	13:00 ~ 14:59
申	Shin Metal	Hour of Monkey	15:00 ~ 16:59
酉	Yoo Metal	Hour of Rooster	17:00 ~ 18:59
戌	Sool Earth	Hour of Dog	19:00 ~ 20:59
亥	Hae Water	Hour of Pig	21:00 ~ 22:59

In ancient societies, a woman in labor had no control over when to deliver her baby; she simply had to let nature take its course. Today, choosing—within reason—the day and the hour of delivery has become an option. When a cesarean section delivery is unavoidable, the mother could consult a saju specialist and choose the most auspicious day and/or hour of birth for her child. This is a normative practice in many cultures where saju reading is a common method of divination, but it is also a controversial practice. The saju consultant who is selecting the most auspicious hour of delivery could be risking possible karmic repercussions by meddling in the infant's destiny. Besides, there is no guarantee that a doctor would be available to deliver the baby in the chosen hour.

On a different note, doctors performing cesarean sections are likely to choose the delivery hour during their normal working hours. This results in a lot of babies being born during the day time, inevitably adding fire energies to their Hour Pillars. Whether this is good or bad should be examined case by case, but statistically, a portion of these babies would end up with excessive fire energies in their saju compositions.

Constructing Your Hour Pillar

If you know the exact time (the hour and minutes) of your birth, you'd know which Earthly Branch to use in your Hour Pillar just by reviewing the time chart above. If you were born at 6am, for instance, you would use 卯 Myo Wood (Hour of Rabbit) for the Earthly Branch slot of your Hour Pillar. Now, the question is which Heavenly Stem should accompany the Branch: This is determined by the Stem representing the Day Master in the saju chart.

If you plan to always use an automated online TTY calendar for pulling up the saju charts, you will never have to calculate and construct the Hour Pillar yourself, since the computer program does it for you. But if you wish to know the theory behind establishing the Hour Pillar, refer to Appendix A at the end of the book.

***

♦Important note on the 子 Jah Water Hour: If you were born any time between 23:00 and 23:59, then your birthday is actually considered to be the following day due to the lateness of the hour, as 11pm through 12:59am is considered the first hour of the day. If you were born at 11:40pm on June 10, then your Hour Pillar should reflect the first hour of June 11 as 子 Jah Water Hour, and your saju chart—your Day Pillar in particular—will be established based on the day of June 11.

***

Chapter 7 Exercise

1. Explore the four Branches in your saju chart. Which Branches appear in your Year, Month, Day, and Hour Pillars? What are the animal signs of the Branches? How do the Branches interact with the Day Master as elements?
2. Explore the Branches in the saju chart(s) of your significant other(s).

Chapter 8 The Sexagenary Cycle

There is a time for everything, and a season for every activity under the heavens.
Ecclesiastes 3:1

The twenty-two Han characters of the Saju Alphabet are derivatives of the Yin-Yang theory and the Five Phases as these theories define each character in terms of its yin-yang energy and elemental nature. The Ten Heavenly Stems as a whole represent the heavenly realm ruled by yang energy; the Twelve Earthly Branches represent the earthly realm ruled by yin energy. The Stems and the Branches together remind us that human survival is dependent on both energies of yin and yang inasmuch as we need our mind and body to live. We require the coordinated function of the mind and the body as one unit in order to continue our existence in a meaningful fashion. Likewise, the Stems and the Branches are inseparable, and they always come in the Stem-Branch combination format.

The Stem-Branch combination begins with the first characters from each group. The combination of the first Heavenly Stem, 甲 Gahp Wood, and the first Earthly Branch, 子 Jah Water, yields the very first Stem-Branch combination: 甲子 (*gahp-jah*). The combined characters can be written vertically or horizontally.

甲子　甲子

Combined together, the Stem-Branch unit offers a story and a meaning. In this first combination of 甲子 (*gahp-jah*), we see a large tree standing on, or surrounded by, a water body. Since Water is the natural nurturer of Wood, the metaphor of "a child with a mother" can be applied to this unit. What does this mean? We can say that the 甲子 unit is a suitable match, for what child would not want to be with his mother? At the same time, however, 子 Jah Water represents the middle of the winter season, with the yin energy of Water reaching its height in frigid temperatures. So, this is really a tree standing on ice or icy water—a tree that is frozen and immobile, apparently requiring fire energy nearby to achieve a sense of balance. In this case, even the nurturing energy of 子 Jah Water can be questionable; what sort of a mother would she be to her child? Perhaps a mother who is cold or stoic, if fire energy is nowhere to be found. Another imagery can be attributed to the 甲子 Stem-Branch unit: a rat (子) roaming around under a large tree (甲). Since 甲 Gahp Wood can also be seen as a loud thunder, we can imagine the rat that is running around in a state of panic. These imageries provide little to big details for understanding the 甲子 unit that can show up in any Pillar in the saju chart. As a rule of thumb, the suitability or the auspiciousness of a Stem-Branch unit must be assessed contextually in relation to other Stems and Branches in the chart.

With Ten Stems and Twelve Branches, there exists a total of sixty Stem-Branch combinations that serve as the building blocks of the Four Pillars. These sixty units make up the Sexagenary Cycle in its entirety. The term sexagenary comes from the Latin word *sexaginta,* meaning "sixty." Given the total number of Stems and Branches, one might think that it would take 120 combinations for all of the Stems to unite with all of the Branches. But there is an important rule to follow: The matched Stem and Branch must share the same yin-yang energy. The first Stem 甲 Gahp Wood comes in yang energy, so it can only be combined with six of the Twelve Branches that are also yang in energy. Hence, only sixty combinations are possible, as yang characters and yin characters do not pair up.

To establish the sixty Stem-Branch combinations of the Sexagenary Cycle, the Heavenly Stems undergo six cycles, and the Earthly Branches undergo five cycles:

The Sexagenary Cycle										Leftover Branches
甲子 1	乙丑 2	丙寅 3	丁卯 4	戊辰 5	己巳 6	庚午 7	辛未 8	壬申 9	癸酉 10	戌亥 *sool, hae*
甲戌 11	乙亥 12	丙子 13	丁丑 14	戊寅 15	己卯 16	庚辰 17	辛巳 18	壬午 19	癸未 20	申酉 *shin, yoo*
甲申 21	乙酉 22	丙戌 23	丁亥 24	戊子 25	己丑 26	庚寅 27	辛卯 28	壬辰 29	癸巳 30	午未 *oh, mee*
甲午 31	乙未 32	丙申 33	丁酉 34	戊戌 35	己亥 36	庚子 37	辛丑 38	壬寅 39	癸卯 40	辰巳 *jin, sah*
甲辰 41	乙巳 42	丙午 43	丁未 44	戊申 45	己酉 46	庚戌 47	辛亥 48	壬子 49	癸丑 50	寅卯 *inn, myo*
甲寅 51	乙卯 52	丙辰 53	丁巳 54	戊午 55	己未 56	庚申 57	辛酉 58	壬戌 59	癸亥 60	子丑 *jah, chook*

Table 8.1

Each row in the Sexagenary Cycle shows all of the Ten Heavenly Stems in their natural sequence. The Stems are combined with the Earthly Branches in the order that they come. The characters in the combined units are compatible in their yin-yang energy since yin and yang always alternate for both sets of the Stems and the Branches. Once the sixtieth unit is in place, the entire cycle is complete, ready to repeat itself.

The Sexagenary Cycle as the Time Keeper

In the absence of Arabic numerals, a long time ago, the Sexagenary Cycle was used for organizing and keeping time. The usage was versatile: It was used to calculate the years, months, days, and hours as reflected in the TTY calendar. Representing the years, the cycle takes 60 years; representing the months, the cycle takes 5 years from start to finish; representing the days, it takes about 2 months; and representing the hours, it takes 5 days. Once a cycle is completed, it simply repeats itself. As such, the Sexagenary Cycle is equivalent to a clock (with four hands!), a time keeper that is informed by the movements of celestial bodies, including the earth rotating and orbiting the sun, and the earth's moon rotating and orbiting the earth.

The Sexagenary Cycle was first used to record dates and times in ancient China. There are records of successive kings of China using the Han characters from the Sexagenary Cycle in their names as early as the eighteenth century BCE. The Sexagenary Cycle is, apparently, a very old clock that never stops. The year 2021, the year of White Ox (辛丑), is number 38 in the cycle. The year 2022 is the year of Black Tiger (壬寅), number 39. The year 2023 is the Year of Black Rabbit (癸卯), number 40 in the cycle. (The animal's color is determined by the element comprising the Stem: Water is black, Fire is red, Wood is green, Metal is white, and Earth is yellow or gold. The animals can also be described by the elements—e.g., Metal Ox, Water Tiger, Water Rabbit, etc).

The 60 Stem-Branch combinations are used to construct the Four Pillars as they correspond to the different units of time in the TTY calendar. They can stand for the Year, Month, Day, and Hour Pillars in any order and in any combination. The number of different saju charts that can possibly be derived from the sixty Stem-Branch combinations is 518,400. (60 Stem-Branch units (in years) x 12 Months x 60 Stem-Branch units (in days) x 12 Hours = 518,400) This is more than a half million different saju compositions, alluding to the diversity of human lives. With 8 billion people around the world, we can assume that approximately 15,432 people would share the same saju composition. (8 billion ÷ 518,400 = 15,432) Would those fifteen thousand and plus people live the exact same lives? Of course, not. Their country, ethnicity, geography, socio-political situation, family of origin, gender, and the genetic makeup of their physique and psychology would have to play a role in defining and shaping their destiny. The saju charts merely serve to offer roadmaps for individual journeys in life.

The Concept of *Gongmang*

On the far-right column of the Sexagenary Cycle (Table 8.1), there are two Earthly Branches without their Heavenly Stem partners in each row. Although these leftover Branches pick up their Stem partners in the next row, that, in turn, results in another set of Branches without their Stem partners for that row. This is because, obviously, there are only ten Heavenly Stems for the Twelve Earthly Branches. When the ten slots are filled by the Ten Stems, two Branches will always remain without any Stem partners for every row. There is a total of six such pairs, as this condition applies to all of the Twelve Branches.

The pair of leftover Branches are called *gong-mang* (空亡) that translates to "empty-ruin." *Gong* means "empty," and *mang* refers to a state of "ruin." *Gong* is associated with the first leftover Branch (yang), and *mang* is associated with the second Branch (yin). *Gongmang* always comes in these pairs.

The concept of *gongmang* is frequently used in saju analysis as every saju is given one pair of *gongmang* Branches. Because *gongmang* refers to the absence of Stem energies for the particular pair of Branches, when these *gongmang* Branches show up in the saju chart or in the luck cycles, they tend to carry a negative connotation. *Gongmang* Branches can never show up in the Day Pillar; they can only occupy other Pillars which yields analytical implications. Occasionally, *gongmang* Branches can function beneficially, especially when an undesirable Branch in the saju chart happens to be a *gongmang* Branch, in which case the negative effects of the undesirable Branch are diminished. This is like double negatives canceling each other out to make a positive.

Again, every saju owner has to deal with a pair of *gongmang* Branches whether they show up in their Four Pillars or not. Your *gongmang* pair is determined by the row your Day Pillar is located on in the Sexagenary Cycle (See Table 8.1). If your Day Pillar is one of the ten Stem-Branch combinations (#1 through #10) in the first row, your *gongmang* pair is 戌亥 (Sool-Hae), the first pair of the leftover Branches. If you find your Day Pillar in the next row (#11 through #20), then your *gongmang* pair is 申酉 (Shin-Yoo), and so forth. There are other ways to determine your *gongmang* pair, but for now, referencing the Sexagenary Cycle table will be convenient. The Sexagenary Cycle and the *gongmang* Branches are listed in Appendix B for reference.

***

Chapter 8 Exercise

1. Find your *gongmang* Branches. How do these Branches relate to your Day Master? Are they controlling, nurturing, or requiring the Day Master's control or nurture?
2. Find the *gongmang* Branches for your significant other(s).

Chapter 9 Four Seasons and Their Subdivisions

Does Heaven ever speak? The four seasons come and go, and all creatures thrive and grow. Does Heaven ever speak!
Confucius

A common theme that runs through the core of sajuology, as we have explored thus far, has to do with the four seasons of the year. The concepts of Five Phases, Ten Heavenly Stems, and Twelve Earthly Branches all revolve around the seasonal changes and their impact on human life. While climatic change has always mattered to humans, a critical event in history had made it even more significant: the emergence of agriculture. About ten thousand years ago, humans began to cultivate the land and develop farming skills, moving on from the hunting and gathering phase of existence. This helped to produce food they could count on. The discovery of agriculture had accelerated the development of civilization as people embraced a more settled way of life by learning to farm, domesticate animals, make home goods, establish religious communities, and build ethnic societies. Farmers were naturally concerned with the climate, since successful farming depended on good weather.

A farmland requires the balance of sun and rain to produce healthy and abundant crops. The ancient sages looked to the sky to study the patterns of sun and heat, rain and cold, and ascertained the seasons for every activity. The heavens proved to be the *clock* they needed to consult in order to determine what time it is to do what on the earth. They sowed in spring and harvested in fall, as crops grew fiercely in summer while the land became dormant in winter. The changing positions of the celestial bodies governed the day and night, and the exact time each season transitioned in the year. The sages witnessed the miracle of the four seasons as the heaven's work of art. They believed in the mighty power of the sun and the subtle strength of the moon. They understood the two contrasting forces of yin and yang, and the critical importance of the two forces in maintaining a balance.

In Northeast Asia, the empirical data gathered from astronomical and agricultural observations led to the development of practical studies including sajuology, fengshuiology, herbal medicine, and acupuncture. Nature's indisputable laws were the basis for these studies. The ancient sages believed that to be human was to be one with nature, since humans are born from nature. In their exploration of the sacred trinity—the heavens, the earth, and human beings—they discovered the secrets of forecasting human destiny.

Inasmuch as the region of Northeast Asia is the birthplace of sajuology, the temperate climate of the region has everything to do with the Four Pillars system. By its barest definition, the Four Pillars method is the study of hot, cold, wet, and dry conditions that manifest over time. Similar to how humans react differently to hot, cold, wet, and dry environments, human destiny takes shape and flow according to the conditions implied in the Four Pillars and its luck cycles.

The Subdivided Seasons

We are familiar with the four seasons being divided into the 12 months of the year. In sajuology, the four seasons are further divided into 24 periods, which highlight the subtle changes in activities of each season. Twelve of these periods mark the precise points of transition from one month to the next.

Seasons	Dates	24 Subdivisions
Spring	Feb. 4 or 5 Feb. 18 or 19 March 5 or 6 March 20 or 21 April 4 or 5 April 20 or 21	#1. *Spring Begins*: Beginning of spring #2. *Rain Water*: Spring rain #3. *Waking of Insects*: Animals awake from hibernation #4. *Spring Equinox*: Day and night are equal in length #5. *Pure Brightness*: Sky is clear #6. *Grain Rain*: Rain water for cultivated fields
Summer	May 5 or 6 May 21 or 22 June 5 or 6 June 21 or 22 July 7 or 8 July 22 or 23	#7. *Summer Begins*: Beginning of summer #8. *Lesser Fullness of Grain*: Nature begins to grow in abundant sunlight #9. *Grain in Beard*: Time to sow the fields with grain seed #10. *Summer Solstice*: Sun is at the highest; longest day and shortest night of the year #11. *Lesser Heat*: Heat begins to increase #12. *Greater Heat*: Heat is at its height following the rainy season
Autumn	Aug. 7 or 8 Aug. 23 or 24 Sept. 7 or 8 Sept. 23 or 24 Oct. 8 or 9 Oct. 23 or 24	#13. *Autumn Begins*: Beginning of autumn #14. *End of Heat*: Heat starts to decrease; diurnal range of temperatures increases #15. *White Dew*: Dew falls with decrease in temperatures #16. *Autumn Equinox*: Night begins to get longer #17. *Cold Dew*: Cool dew falls in height of harvest activities #18. *Frost's Descent*: Frost begins to fall; crimson foliage of autumn leaves is at its height
Winter	Nov. 7 or 8 Nov. 22 or 23 Dec. 7 or 8 Dec. 21 or 22 Jan. 5 or 6 Jan. 20 or 21	#19. *Winter Begins*: Beginning of winter #20. *Lesser Snow*: Ice begins to form in cold weather #21. *Greater Snow*: Snow season is at its height #22. *Winter Solstice*: Shortest day and longest night of the year #23. *Lesser Cold*: Winter's coldest season #24. *Greater Cold*: Cold begins to dwindle

The significance of the 24 subdivisions is that they override the dates on the lunar calendar. In other words, the numbered subdivisions dictate the demarcation from one lunar month to the next, regardless of what the calendar month dates say. This information is important when you are using the hard copy version of the TTY calendar. (Users of the digital TTY calendar need not be concerned about the seasonal demarcation dates.)

The twelve cutoff points—all odd numbered subdivisions—between the lunar months come as follows:

Lunar Month		Subdivisions	Solar Month
寅	Inn Wood	#1 Spring Begins	February
卯	Myo Wood	#3 Waking of Insects	March
辰	Jin Earth	#5 Pure Brightness	April
巳	Sah Fire	#7 Summer Beginns	May
午	Oh Fire	#9 Grain in Beard	June
未	Mee Earth	#11 Lesser Heat	July
申	Shin Metal	#13 Autumn Begins	August
酉	Yoo Metal	#15 White Dew	September
戌	Sool Earth	#17 Cold Dew	October
亥	Hae Water	#19 Winter Begins	November
子	Jah Water	#21 Greater Snow	December
丑	Chook Earth	#23 Lesser Cold	January

Based on the subdivided dates, February 1 is not exactly the beginning of the 寅 Inn Wood month; the Month of Tiger starts on the day of subdivided season *#1 Spring Begins,* that usually lands on February 4 or 5. The Chinese New Year Day is generally considered as the beginning of the new lunar year, but this day also must fall on *Spring Begins* in order to truly mark the beginning of the new year. For instance, the Chinese New Year Day in 2022 was on February 1, but the day of *Spring Begins* was on February 4; thus, the new year actually began on February 4 in 2022.

Ascertaining the actual demarcation dates is important when it comes to constructing the Month Pillar of the saju chart. For example, I was born on the month of 戌 Sool Earth according to the hard copy version of the TTY calendar, but because my birthday is at the end of that month, and because the *Beginning of Winter* came one day before my birthday, my Month Pillar reflects the following month of 亥 Hae Water. The subdivided season *#19 Beginning of Winter* is the demarcation point between the 戌 Sool Earth and the 亥 Hae Water months. There are saju readers who would take this information differently. One side insisted that I use 戌 Sool Earth for my Month Pillar since my birthday falls on that month according to the calendar; the other side insisted that I use 亥 Hae Water month because my birthday comes one day after the *Beginning of Winter* that marks the beginning of 亥 Hae Water month. I chose the 亥 Hae Water month, not only because the interpretations fit better, but using the time of seasonal change is theoretically correct. Changes in seasons—and the conditions they bring—matter the most when constructing the Four Pillars for an evaluation.

***

♦Online saju calculators, if programmed correctly, will build your Four Pillars according to the subdivided seasons as these are integral aspects of all TTY calendars.

Chapter 10 The Luck Cycles

Being deeply learned and skilled, being well trained and using well spoken words: this is good luck.
Buddha

Working with the set of luck cycles uniquely generated by a saju chart is an integral component of saju analysis. The luck cycles that are 10 years in length—the most important ones—are called the Larger Luck cycles, and there are 5-year, 1-year, monthly, daily, and hourly luck cycles that are relevant to everyday living. Daily and hourly luck cycles matter when you wish to choose the most auspicious day or time for holding special events such as a wedding or a surgery. By comparison, the 10-year, 5-year, 1-year, and monthly luck cycles, and any special combination of these, have a broader impact on our lives. The matryoshka, the Russian nested doll set, is a helpful imagery. The dolls come in several sizes, and the smaller dolls can fit inside the larger dolls. Likewise, there are daily luck cycles in the monthly luck cycles that are included in the one-year luck cycle, which is part of the 5-year, and finally the 10-year luck cycles. The overlapping luck cycles can create a powerful force to bring good or harm when their particular combination is designed to generate a great synergy.

The 10-year luck cycles, referred to as the Larger Luck cycles, are unique to each saju chart, and their particular sequence is determined by the Month Pillar in the chart. The Larger Luck Cycle sequence (LLCS) is automatically calculated when you pull up your saju chart using a digital saju calculator or an app. The LLCS is ordered from birth to about age hundred, and it is a built-in feature for all saju charts. You must input your gender to access your saju chart because the LLCS calculation is dependent on the person's gender. If a man and a woman input identical birthdate information, they will output different sets of LLCS due to their gender difference. Choosing the gender to input can become tricky for those who have changed their gender in the course of their life. They may use the gender assigned to them at birth, but ultimately, this has to be a personal choice. Outputting both sets of LLCS (one for female and one for male) can be an option, though it will take more time to evaluate both sets for a single saju chart.

The LLCS moves in the order of the sixty Stem-Branch combinations of the Sexagenary Cycle. So, it has a distinct flow and is never lined up randomly. For some saju charts, the LLCS flows in a forward direction—in the order of the sequence reflected in the Sexagenary Cycle. In other saju charts, the LLCS flows backward, in the backward direction of the flow in the Sexagenary Cycle. In either case, the luck cycles are always in motion, always changing over time. Fortunate and less fortunate lucks come and go, and we can choose to work with them in the manner that best suits our needs once we know what they are.

Calculating the Larger Luck Cycle Sequence

There are rules to follow when establishing the LLCS. If you are using a digital saju calculator, you don't have to construct the LLCS yourself as it will be automatically generated. So, this is a technical piece of information you may or may not have to use.

1. Your Month Pillar determines the beginning Pillar of your LLCS, with reference to the sixty Stem-Branch combinations lined up in the Sexagenary Cycle.
2. The beginning age for the LLCS can be found in the TTY calendar. A digital saju calculator will automatically generate and indicate the ages right above the luck cycle pillars. The smallest number is the earliest age your

10-year luck cycle begins to take effect. (Female and male with an identical saju will have different beginning ages.)

3. The sequence for females born in the yin year moves in a forward direction; the sequence for females born in the yang year moves in a backward direction.

4. The sequence for males born in the yang year moves in a forward direction; the sequence for males born in the yin year moves in a backward direction.

5. If the sequence is to move in a forward direction, the first Larger Luck cycle in the sequence is the Stem-Branch unit that comes *after* the Month Pillar and the whole sequence is to move in that direction.

6. If the sequence is moving in a backward direction, the first Larger Luck cycle in the sequence is the Stem-Branch unit that comes *before* the Month Pillar and the whole sequence is to move in that direction.

Evaluating the Luck Cycles

A luck cycle always comes in the form of a pillar, equipped with a Stem and a Branch, and it can be any one of the sixty Stem-Branch units. Evaluating your luck cycle is crucial to understanding your life's journey, and it can answer the questions that matter to you in relation to the time frame indicated by the luck cycles. Begin with the following guideline when evaluating your luck cycles whether they represent the 10-year, 5-year, 1-year, monthly, daily or hourly luck.

1. Ascertain the elements, yin-yang energy, and the Stem-Branch characters comprising the luck cycle.

2. Examine how the luck cycle interacts with the Day Pillar of the saju, especially the Day Master. Juxtapose the luck cycle next to the saju chart as a "fifth pillar" to assess how it fits in the overall composition.

3. Focus on the luck cycle's effect on the well-being of the Day Master. Does it support or challenge the Day Master?

How does it support or challenge the Day Branch? Does it disturb or offer balance in the saju composition? Does it create any harmonious merger or conflicting clash with the characters in the chart?

4. Recall the matryoshka doll set. A luck cycle is never without a context. If a luck cycle in question is the yearly luck cycle, it should be evaluated within the context of the Larger Luck cycle that shows the 10-year and the 5-year cycles. Hence, you are working with several Stem-Branch units all at once when exploring the various luck cycles and their concerted effect on the saju composition.

A Case Study

This is an example of a LLCS generated by a saju chart. This chart belongs to the thirty-fifth president of the US, John F. Kennedy, who was born on May 29, 1917 in Brookline, Massachusetts, around 3pm.

Hour	Day	Month	Year
乙	辛	乙	丁
eul yin wood	*shin* yin metal	*eul* yin wood	*jeong* yin fire
未	未	巳	巳
mee yin earth	*mee* yin earth	*sah* yin fire	*sah* yin fire

98	88	78	68	58	48	38	28	18	8
乙	丙	丁	戊	己	庚	辛	壬	癸	甲
- wood	+ fire	- fire	+ earth	- earth	+ metal	- metal	+ water	- water	+ wood
未	申	酉	戌	亥	子	丑	寅	卯	辰
- earth	+ metal	- metal	+ earth	- water	+ water	- earth	+ wood	- wood	+ earth

J. F. Kennedy is a male born in the yin year of 巳 Sah Fire, the Year of Red Snake (丁巳), so his LLCS is flowing backward, starting from the 甲辰 Stem-Branch unit (#41) that comes *before* the 乙巳 unit (#42) that is occupying his Month Pillar. The beginning age of his LLC sequence is indicated as 8, or the eighth year from his birth year (so, it is actually age 7).

From 18 (age 17), Kennedy is under the influence of 癸卯 cycle, which is #40 in the Sexagenary Cycle. Since 28 (age 27), he is under the influence of 壬寅 cycle (#39), and so on. Kennedy died at the end of his 辛丑 Larger Luck cycle at the age of 46, and did not live to see the rest of the 10-year luck cycles in the sequence.

The 5-year luck cycles are conveyed by the two characters—the Heavenly Stem and the Earthly Branch—making up the Larger Luck cycle. The first 5 years are under the influence of the Heavenly Stem portion; the following 5 years are under the influence of the Earthly Branch. This makes the 5-year luck cycle a single character that is either a Stem or a Branch; the 5-year cycle is thus unique in that it is not a whole pillar like other luck cycles.

The two 5-year luck cycles embedded in the 辛丑 Larger Luck cycle (fourth in the sequence), which governed Kennedy's life between the ages of 37 and 46, were a favorable time for Kennedy. The 5-year luck of 辛 Shin Metal, being the same Stem as the Day Master, naturally augmented the strength of Kennedy's weak Day Master. In addition, the 5-year luck of 丑 Chook Earth offered the much-needed nurturing energy to the 辛 Shin Metal Day Master.

Hour	Day	Month	Year	4th LLC
乙	辛	乙	丁	辛
eul yin wood	*shin* yin metal	*eul* yin wood	*jeong* yin fire	*shin* yin metal
未	未	巳	巳	丑
mee yin earth	*mee* yin earth	*sah* yin fire	*sah* yin fire	*chook* yin earth

The 5-year luck period controlled by the 丑 Chook Earth Branch (age 42 to 46) was especially auspicious for Kennedy as he was elected to be the US president during this time. This was the only time that one of his Larger Luck cycles truly empowered him, given his saju composition with the 辛 Shin Metal Day Master that is facing several challenges. Kennedy's saju chart shows a prolific presence of yin Fire energy with one 丁 Jeong Fire and two 巳 Sah Fires that are poised to heavily control the yin Metal Day Master. But, with the emergence of 丑 Chook Earth as a 5-year luck cycle, the two 巳 Sah Fires harmoniously interact with the 丑 Chook Earth to create a wide spread of metal energy, thus exponentially enhancing the power of the Day Master. This is equivalent to finding your worst enemies suddenly becoming your best allies. When this auspicious luck cycle had reached its end, the president was assassinated. He died just 2 months short of his next 10-year luck cycle of 庚子, the fifth Larger Luck cycle in the sequence.

The yearly luck cycles that are contained in the 5-year luck cycle simply represent the calendar years. They are not unique to a given saju; everyone has the same yearly luck cycles sequenced according to the TTY calendar. The year 1963 was the Year of Black Rabbit, expressed as 癸卯 Gyeh-Myo yearly luck cycle. In that year, the first 6 months were under the influence of the Heavenly Stem, 癸 Gyeh Water; and the latter half of the year was under the influence of the Earthly Branch, 卯 Myo Wood. Kennedy's 辛 Shin Metal Day Master is the natural nemesis of 卯 Myo Wood, as in yin metal clashing with yin wood. This encounter resembles two kings from the opposite territories fighting the final fight. The saju owner (the 辛 Shin Metal Day Master) was defeated later that year, in the month of 亥 Hae Water (November)—a monthly luck cycle that had augmented the lethal power of 卯 Myo Wood (through a harmonious merger) against the 辛 Shin Metal Day Master.

Evaluating Kennedy's saju composition, I pondered on a couple of questions: What if he hadn't traveled to the south (the direction of fire energy)? What if it wasn't at noon (the Hour of 午 Oh Fire) that he had greeted the public in an open car? A weak 辛 Shin Metal (yin metal) Day Master must avoid yin fire (lethal heat) and yin wood (ominous clash) whenever possible. In order to protect its well-being and to gain strength, it needs the help of Metal (peer support) and Earth (nurturing energy). 辛 Shin Metals can also appreciate the presence of Water if the saju composition is excessively hot or dry as in the case of Kennedy's. If he had survived that fateful day in November, he would have done well for, at the least, another 10 years with the Larger Luck cycle of 庚子 that would have prolonged the life of the 辛 Shin Metal Day Master by offering the much-needed metal and water energy.

Four Pillars vs. Luck Cycles

The writer of Ecclesiastes states, "There is a time for everything, and a season for every activity under the heavens." (Eccles. 3:1) The LLCS that accompanies the saju chart reveals the different seasons in our lives. Knowing the seasons and the timely activities for the seasons can help us to manage our lives better. The time to study, the time to marry, the time to travel abroad, the time to expand business, the time to rest, the time to step up to the challenging circumstances and the likes are part of the seasons presented by the luck cycles.

So, which is more important? Your saju or your luck cycles? There are two camps with differing views. One camp believes that the construct of the saju is more important, because the *power* to take on the luck cycles originates from it. For example, a vehicle like a Hummer can perform well on most road conditions as a sturdy, versatile SUV, and if you have a saju like a Hummer, you have little to fear when challenging luck cycles head your way. Proponents of this camp contend that the saju composition determines the outcome of the luck cycles, just as the capabilities of a vehicle determine the outcome of the journey.

Those in the opposite camp believe that the luck cycles matter more than the saju composition, because no matter how balanced and well equipped a saju is, it is still vulnerable to the inauspicious luck cycles that can interact with the Four Pillars to cause ill-fated disruptions. Even a Hummer can end up in tatters after traveling on deserts, mountains, and on icy roads long enough. The inauspicious luck cycles are like the birth pangs: when they come, they will come and they will do what they have to do, and you will simply have to ride them out, hoping for the best nonetheless. There seems to be an aspect of inevitability to human destiny not so different from death and taxes.

It seems that both camps offer compelling arguments. But it is true that there are more saju scholars siding with the latter perspective in that one's luck cycles are more important in shaping one's destiny. I like to think that both the saju and the luck cycles hold equal importance; but as an advocate of faith and spiritual practices, I also believe in the transcendental power of human beings to rise above their fate when earnest efforts are made to do so.

***

Chapter 10 Exercise

1. Examine your LLCS (lined up under your saju chart). At what age does your first 10-year luck cycle take effect? Examine the flow of your sequence.
2. Examine the LLCS of your significant other(s).

Chapter 11 The Hidden-Stems in the Branches

Heaven is under our feet as well as over our heads.
Henry David Thoreau

The Earthly Branches represent energies of the earthly realm; however, they are not entirely separate from the Stem energies of the heavenly realm. This brings us to the Hidden-Stems-in-Branch theory that introduces another dimension of the Earthly Branches.

To begin, let's compare the air in the sky and the soil on the earth. The sky is wide open and airy, and nothing is hidden there. These are the characteristics of yang energy. The earth's soil, on the other hand, is dense, hidden in layers and not so transparent. These are the characteristics of yin energy. The dualistic view of heaven and earth portrays them as two completely different entities. From the soil's point of view, however, it is constantly affected by the energies coming from the sky. Rain comes from the sky and wets the earth. Hot, cold, and dry winds come from the sky and alter the condition of the soil. During the snowing season, the earth becomes hard and frozen. From these phenomena, the Hidden-Stems-in-Branch theory was born. This is a theory commonly used in saju interpretation; advanced saju readers will interpret the Hidden-Stems in addition to the eight characters of the Four Pillars and provide an added layer of insight and understanding.

The Earthly Branches as the 12 Months

The Hidden-Stems-in-Branch theory involves using the Twelve Earthly Branches as the twelve months of the year. The theory states that there are three Stems hidden in each Branch, based on their commonly shared elements. The "pure" Branches have only two Hidden-Stems.

The three Hidden-Stems in each Branch can be categorized into three types of energy that transpire each month:

1. Type 1: Residual energy from the previous month.
2. Type 2-1: Lingering energy from the previous season — this applies to the Earth Phase Branches only.
3. Type 2-2: Potential energy for the next season — this applies to the Wood, Fire, Metal, and Water Phase Branches only.
4. Type 3: Dominant energy of the month.

The three types of energies only last for a certain number of days within the month. The number of days is organized into: 1) the beginning period; 2) the middle period; and 3) the dominant period.

The Beginning Period

Each Branch representing a month accommodates some residual energy from the previous month in its beginning period. Energies don't change at once just because the calendar month has changed. The carried over energies last between 7 to 10 days, depending on the Branch. 亥 Hae Water Branch, for instance, harbors 戊 Moo Earth (yang Earth) in the beginning for 7 days, since it follows the month of 戌 Sool Earth (yang Earth). The presence of different Stems hidden inside the Branches apparently adds to their complexity, but also adds versatility and potency to the Branches.

The Middle Period

We must understand the Earth Phase Branches differently from other Branches when we examine their middle periods. The four Earth Branches are the ones carrying the *previous season's energy* in their middle periods. This grants them the function of a *storage*, since the previous season's energies in the Branches are being stored up for several months. The energy stored inside the middle period of an Earth Branch *halts all its activity* for the duration of those months. This is the Earth Branches' way of contributing to make the environment suitable for the coming of the next season—since the stored-up energy is an element that would clash with the energy of the next season.

In line with the Earth Branches' efforts to promote the upcoming season, the other Branches—Fire, Wood, Metal, and Water—harbor the *potential* energy for the upcoming season in their middle periods. The energies occupying the middle period of each month last between 3 to 9 days, depending on the Branch.

The Dominant Period
The dominant period represents the actual energy of the given month, according to the Branch's element and yin-yang energy. For instance, the month of 申 Shin Metal (yang Metal) has 庚 Kyoung Metal (yang Metal) in its dominant period; the given Branch and Stem share the same element as well as the same yin-yang energy. The dominant periods last between 11 to 20 days each month, depending on the Branch.

A Review of the Four Seasons
Revisiting the four seasons of the year will be helpful before we continue to explore the Hidden-Stems in the Branches. The four seasons come in the order of Wood, Fire, Metal, and Water as spring, summer, autumn, and winter, respectively. The four Earth Phase months technically do not represent a season per se, and they play a supportive role by serving as the transitional months. Meanwhile, they are still grouped together with the Branches that represent a season, thus their elemental identity (Earth) is compromised, in order to follow the elemental energy of the season.

Spring, the Season of Wood Energy

- 寅 Inn Wood starts off the season of spring in February.
- 卯 Myo Wood marks the height of spring in March.
- 辰 Jin Earth serves as the transitional month in April. It stows Water from the previous season of winter in preparation for summer.

Summer, the Season of Fire Energy

- 巳 Sah Fire marks the beginning of summer in May.
- 午 Oh Fire maintains the heat of summer throughout June.
- 未 Mee Earth serves as the transitional month in July. July is the hottest month of the year due to the accumulated heat energy of the summer months. It stows Wood from the previous season of winter in preparation for autumn.

Autumn, the Season of Metal Energy

- 申 Shin Metal marks the beginning of autumn in August.
- 酉 Yoo Metal indicates the height of autumn in September.
- 戌 Sool Earth serves as the transitional month in October. It stows Fire from the previous season of summer in preparation for winter.

Winter, the Season of Water Energy

- 亥 Hae Water marks the beginning of winter in November.
- 子 Jah Water indicates the height of winter in December.
- 丑 Chook Earth serves as the transitional month in January. January is the coldest month of the year due to the accumulated coldness of the winter months. It stows Metal from the previous season of autumn in preparation for spring.

***

The storage function of the Earth Phase Earthly Branches is an important concept to remember for analytical purposes. The Hidden-Stems these Branches store in their middle periods formally define their storage name, even though they carry other Hidden-Stems in their beginning and dominant periods. This is because what they "store" dictates their mutability as Branches. For example, 戌 Sool Earth is the Earth Branch from the season of autumn that carries a good amount of metal energy in its beginning period, but it is formally known as the Storage of Fire since it carries (briefly for just 3 days) fire energy from the previous season of summer in its middle period. This hint of fire energy plays an important role, giving 戌 Sool Earth the potential to transform into Fire when combined with the right set of Branches. Likewise, all other Earth Branches are highly mutational. This is reflective of the flexible nature of the neutral Earth Branches. If you are neutral, you are more likely to take a side when the opportunity is given. Hence, saju charts that have one or more Earth Branch require special attention in light of their mutability.

Branch Months	Hidden Stems	Beginning Period		Middle Period		Beginning Period	
寅 February		戊	7 days	丙	7 days	甲	16 days
卯 March		甲	10 days			乙	20 days
辰 April		乙	9 days	癸	3 days	戊	18 days
巳 May		戊	7 days	庚	7 days	丙	16 days
午 June		丙	10 days	己	9 days	丁	11 days
未 July		丁	9 days	乙	3 days	己	18 days
申 August		戊	7 days	壬	7 days	庚	16 days
酉 September		庚	10 days			辛	20 days
戌 October		辛	9 days	丁	3 days	戊	18 days
亥 November		戊	7 days	甲	7 days	壬	16 days
子 December		壬	10 days			癸	20 days
丑 January		癸	9 days	辛	3 days	己	18 days

Table 11.1 The Hidden-Stems-in-Branches

The Branches are like the tip of the iceberg and their Hidden-Stems are like the iceberg beneath the water. Though a saju is made up of eight characters across the Four Pillars, there are, apparently, more characters to attend to when we think of the Hidden-Stems inside the Branches. The Hidden-Stems are equivalent to a root system under the soil; they are not immediately visible, but they have their function, which is to define and support their Branch and to covertly interact with the Day Master.

The Pure and the Not So Pure

There are three "pure" Branches with just two Hidden-Stems instead of three. They are: 子 Jah Water, 卯 Myo Wood, and 酉 Yoo Metal. They are the kings of winter, spring, and autumn, and they are purely made up of a single element—water, wood, and metal, respectively. These "pure" Branches have a beginning and a dominant period without a middle period.

Looking at this list of the "pure" Branches, you may wonder where the king of summer is. The Branch 午 Oh Fire stands for summer as its king, but it is not considered "pure," because it has a middle period with the Hidden-Stem 己 Ghee Earth that doesn't seem to represent the seasonal energy of fire. There is a reason for this anomaly: Because there is such a great amount of heat energy accumulated during summer, the transitional month of 未 Mee Earth alone is not enough to process the heat; it needs help to make sure the heat is tamed adequately before autumn arrives. Hence, 9 days of 己 Ghee Earth is hidden inside the 午 Oh Fire to help process the heat early on prior to the 未 Mee Earth month. In other words, the Hidden Earth Stem starts working early following summer because it is the most energetic season out of the four, necessitating a longer transitional period.

Another Side of the Water and Fire Branches

Table 11.1 shows that the Hidden-Stem occupying the dominant period of a Branch tends to match the yin-yang energy of the Branch. If it is a yang Branch, the dominant energy of the month is represented by a yang Stem. If it is a yin Branch, the dominant energy occupying the month is a yin Stem.

There are four Branches that don't follow this rule. They are 亥 Hae Water, 子 Jah Water, 巳 Sah Fire, and 午 Oh Fire—the first two from winter as yin and yang Waters and the latter two from summer as yin and yang Fires. Table 11.1 reveals that their dominant energies, based on their Hidden-Stems, do not match the original energy of the Branches. The following table summarizes this point:

Earthly Branch	Original Energy	Dominant Energy	Usage in Interpretation
亥 Hae water	yin	yang	yang
子 Jah water	yang	yin	yin
巳 Sah Fire	yin	yang	yang
午 Oh Fire	yang	yin	yin

Table 11.2

In saju analysis, these four Branches are interpreted based on their dominant Hidden-Stem energy. So, 亥 Hae Water is interpreted as yang Water, and 子 Jah Water as yin Water regardless of their originally endowed energy. The same changes apply to the Fire Branches: 巳 Sah Fire is interpreted as yang and 午 Oh Fire as yin.

Applying the Hidden-Stems-in-Branch Theory

The Hidden-Stems indicate the transformative process of seasonal energies moving through the Branches on the monthly basis. The activities of the Stems underneath the earth reveal that there is a more complex set of energies moving in and out in precise patterns so that we can observe and experience the perfect seasons every time.

The Hidden-Stems-in-Branch theory is applicable whenever the Earthly Branches are used; it applies to the Four Pillars and all pillars of the luck cycles. The theory enables us to engage the saju chart on a deeper level; it can even offer hope to the saju owner when a direly needed element is found hidden inside the Branch. Let's say you are in need of fire energy because your saju is lacking in it, and your upcoming Larger Luck cycle is 壬寅, a combination of Water Stem and Wood Branch. Does this mean you're out of luck? Not really, because Table 11.1 shows the presence of 丙 Byoung Fire in the middle period of 寅 Inn Wood. Why does 寅 Inn Wood have a 丙 Byoung Fire hidden inside it? This is because the seed of summer is embedded in 寅 Inn Wood as an indication of the beginning of the next season—that summer with all of its fire energy is on its way. This is a message of hope if you have been waiting for fire energy to enter your life. Summer isn't far away when spring has come.

***

♦ When using an online saju calculator, you may or may not get the list of Hidden-Stems for your saju chart; this depends on the website or the app you're using. It will be helpful to have the Hidden-Stems readily accessible so you have the information when you need it. The Hidden-Stems Table is provided in Appendix C for reference.

***

Chapter 11 Exercise

1. Explore the Hidden-Stems in your chart. Do you find them to be helpful to your Day Master or not?

2. Explore the Hidden-Stems in the charts of your significant other(s).

Chapter 12 Dynamics of the Heavenly Stems

The energy or active exercise of the mind constitutes life.
Aristotle

The Ten Heavenly Stems draw their elemental identity from the yin and yang versions of the Five Phases. As a set of different elements, the Stems are destined to interact with each other to produce either a harmonious or a conflictual condition; and how they attract and repel one another generates analytical implications. The dynamics of the Ten Stems can be divided into two activities: 1) the harmonious interaction where two Stems are attracted to each other, and 2) the clashing interaction where two Stems are in conflict with each other.

The Sixth Conjunctions

Since two Stems are exclusively attracted to each other, the Ten Stems make a total of five pairs of harmonious mergers. One way to find these pairs is to number the Stems in order from one to five, twice, then simply match the Stems with the same numbers.

1	2	3	4	5	1	2	3	4	5
yang wood	yin wood	yang fire	yin fire	yang earth	yin earth	yang metal	yin metal	yang water	yin water
甲	乙	丙	丁	戊	己	庚	辛	壬	癸
gahp	eul	byoung	jeong	moo	ghee	kyoung	shin	yim	gyeh

Matching same numbered Stems yields five harmonious pairs:

1. 甲己 : yang wood and yin earth yields Earth energy
2. 乙庚 : yin wood and yang metal yields Metal energy

121

3. 丙辛 : yang fire and yin metal yields Water energy
4. 丁壬 : yin fire and yang water yields Wood energy
5. 戊癸 : yang earth and yin water yields Fire energy

Each harmonious pair has one yang and one yin element, and yields an element unique to their merger. This resembles a male and a female producing an offspring together. It is important that the two merging Stems stand next to each other in the saju chart for this interaction to take place with full effect. If they are separated by one Pillar standing between them, the effect is lessened; if they are separated by two Pillars, the effect is minimal. Special attention should be given when one of the merging Stems is the Day Master.

As listed above, what the merging Stems produce together can be a completely different, third element, or an amplified version of one of the merging Stems. The final products of the five pairs are the Five Phases in the order of their nurturing relationship. Because the Stems always pair up harmoniously with every sixth Stem, these pairs are called the "sixth conjunctions."

The Seventh Oppositions

The harmonious Stem pairs come in the yin-yang combinations, but the Stems in the clashing pairs share the same yin-yang energy. Opposites attract while identicals repel, like the way the poles of a magnet behave. The Heavenly Stems always clash with every seventh Stem, so they are called the "seventh oppositions." Not all seventh oppositions are considered as the clashing pairs, though. There are four traditionally recognized clashing pairs, and the rest of the six pairs have controlling relationships between the Stems. The clashing pairs portend a harsher outcome than the controlling pairs in saju analysis.

The Clashing Pairs:
1. 甲庚: yang wood clashes with yang metal
2. 乙辛: yin wood clashes with yin metal

3. 丙壬: yang fire clashes with yang water
4. 丁癸: yin fire clashes with yin water
The Controlling Pairs:
5. 戊甲: yang earth is controlled by yang wood
6. 己乙: yin earth is controlled by yin wood
7. 庚丙: yang metal is controlled by yang fire
8. 辛丁: yin metal is controlled by yin fire
9. 壬戊: yang water is controlled by yang earth
10. 癸己: yin water is controlled by yin earth

There are no byproducts for the clashing Stems. These Stems are trying to cancel each other out, much less produce anything together. The four clashing pairs include Wood clashing with Metal, and Fire clashing with Water, and the Stems in the pair must have the same yin-yang energy. The clashing effect is greatest when the two Stems are standing next to each other in the saju chart. If they are separated by one Pillar, the effect is lessened; if they are separated by two Pillars, the effect is minimal.

For the Stem pairs where one is controlling the other, the basic relational properties of the Five Elements apply. The fact that these pairs share the same yin-yang energy still makes this relationship a very difficult one for the Stem that is being controlled. The effect of the controlling relationship is usually a prolonged one, and has a component of consistency; in other words, the suffering may not be overtly noticeable or immediate, but it is there consistently, over an extended period of time—or the time frame suggested by the saju chart or the luck cycles. The effect of a clashing relationship, by comparison, tends to be more immediate and impactful; a clashing effect can easily materialize as significant health problems, deterioration of relationships, or serious accidents. It should be noted that the Stems *can* welcome and collaborate well with their controllers of *opposite* yin-yang energy, as demonstrated by the sixth conjunction pairs.

Usage in Interpretation

The concepts of the sixth conjunction and the seventh opposition are used frequently in saju interpretation. When a sixth conjunction pair is found in the saju chart, the two merging Stems either change into one existing element or create an entirely new element. This is an important distinction and calls for a closer examination.

1. When two Stems merge into one existing element: The 甲 己 and the 乙庚 mergers apply. In the case of the first pair, the wood energy of 甲 Gahp Wood is compromised as it follows the lead of 己 Ghee Earth to produce earth energy together. In the case of the second pair, the wood energy of 乙 Eul Wood is compromised as it follows the lead of 庚 Kyoung Metal to produce metal energy.

2. When two Stems merge to create an entirely new element: The 丙辛, 丁壬, and 戊癸 mergers apply. The powerful 丙 Byoung Fire is seen as melting the 辛 Shin Metal to yield water energy together; the heat and humidity of 丁 Jeong Fire and 壬 Yim Water yield wood energy; and the dry 戊 Moo Earth and wet 癸 Gyeh Water yield fire energy (when the sun shines through a drop of water that functions as a magnifying glass, intense heat is produced on the dry grounds.) The merging Stems do not entirely lose their elemental identity just because they are producing a new element together; but the newly created element enters the scene like a third Stem, wielding its influence in the saju chart.

If harmonious Stem pairs are not found in the saju chart, you still need to pay attention to the Stems lined up in the luck cycles and determine the time frame for any sixth conjunction pairs taking place, as this can yield analytical implications. Working with the luck cycles involves examining their interaction with the Day Pillar (especially the Day Master), watching out for any mergers and clashes. The luck cycle's interaction with the other Pillars in the chart should still be noted, since any significant merger or clash can affect the living environment of the saju owner, including the well-being of one's family members.

The term "harmony" gives off a positive vibe as if it were something to seek out. Then, should all harmonious pairs be welcomed? This depends on the construct of the saju composition. A harmonious merger can be advantageous if it yields an element that is beneficial to balancing the saju and supporting the Day Master. A harmonious merger can also be disadvantageous if it takes a useful Stem element to change it into something else that may not be so useful.

During a compatibility analysis between two people, seeking out for the harmonious pairs between the two sajus is a common practice. The more harmonious pairs there are, the more likely the two people will establish a good rapport. Two Day Stems creating a harmonious pair is considered to be most auspicious. By the same token, discovery of clashing pairs between the two sajus forewarns of potential conflict, especially if the clashing pairs are formed between the same Pillars. Two Day Stems clashing with each other is considered most inauspicious, unless there are other Stem or Branch characters in the two saju charts that are interacting positively to lessen or defuse this clashing effect.

In general, the clashing pairs squarely situated in the saju composition foster an air of disruption. As a rule of thumb, having clashing Stems standing next to each other is not desirable. People with multiple or overlapping clashing Stem pairs may be prone to having "clashing" thought patterns that may affect their personalities. (While the clashing effects of the Heavenly Stems tend to be metaphysical in nature, the physical head area of the person can also be affected, as in recurring headaches.) In some cases, the formation of clashing pairs as a result of engaging the luck cycles can actually do good instead of harm, if a Stem in the luck cycle clashes with the Stem in the saju that has been making the saju owner's life miserable.

Both the harmonious pairs (the sixth conjunctions) and the clashing pairs (the seventh oppositions) can offer advantages and disadvantages depending on their function in the saju layout. Ability to quickly recognize these pairs is important for interpretation purposes.

Examples of Merging and Clashing Stems

The following saju chart belongs to a well-known actor, Harrison Ford, who was born on July 13, 1942. His hour of birth is not revealed to the public, so the Hour Pillar contains no information. The actor's chart shows an example of the harmonious merger of Stems where 丁壬 —yin Fire and yang Water—are interacting to create wood energy together. Due to the presence of two 丁 Jeong Fires, the harmonious interaction is taking place twice, as 壬 Yim Water in the Year Pillar is interacting with both Stems in the Day and Month Pillars.

Hour	Day	Month	Year
?	丁	丁	壬
	jeong yin fire	*jeong* yin fire	*yim* yang water
?	卯	未	午
	myo yin wood	*mee* yin earth	*oh* yang fire

An Example of Merging Stems

The effect of the 丁壬 merger comes with both advantages and disadvantages in the case of Ford's chart. On one side, the newly created wood energy—the outcome of the 丁壬 merger—is naturally supportive of the 丁 Jeong Fire Day Master as its nurturer; it adds character to the practical and sensitive 丁

Day Master, by contributing the qualities of a Wood Stem that includes leadership skills, charisma, strength, and power. The added wood energy allows the 丁Day Master to take his work/career (the "Output" represented by the Month Branch, 未 Mee Earth) and turn it into a profitable enterprise. The downside of the 丁壬 merger is the diminished role of 壬 Yim Water in the saju chart. With three Fires and one fiery Earth spread out across the three Pillars, this saju composition needs the works of Water to achieve a balance. If cold to cool characters (as in Water or Metal) are found in the Hour Pillar to balance the saju, the diminished function of the 壬 Yim Water may not be all that problematic, but without knowing that, a weakened 壬 Yim Water from the 丁壬 merger is considered disadvantageous in the case of Ford's saju composition.

JF Kennedy's saju chart that was introduced in Chapter 10 contains a good example of the clashing Stems. In the chart, we see the 辛 Shin Metal Day Master clashing with two 乙 Eul Wood Stems in the Month and Hour Pillars.

An Example of Clashing Stems

The 乙 Eul Woods clashing from both sides are detrimental to the 辛 Shin Metal Day Master; the harmful effect is squarely on the head of the saju owner—amounting to health issues in the head, and/or conflicting thought patterns. It is interesting that Kennedy had made the remark, "If I don't have sex every day,

I get a headache," (nypost.com) because the two 乙 Eul Woods represent both money and women to the male 辛 Day Master. His frank statement harbors a need to subdue the clashing effect of the 乙 Eul Woods by "conquering" them. The only upside in the case of Kennedy's saju is that the 辛 Day Master is a much stronger element than the two 乙 Eul Woods that are already enervated by so much fire energy in the chart. Still, the clashing effect of the Stems remains at large, and this would go on to affect the life of the saju owner indefinitely, unless a 庚 Kyoung Metal shows up in the luck cycles to merge with the 乙 Eul Woods to yield metal energy, in which case the clashing effect would cease for the duration of time determined by the luck cycle. (It was unfortunate that Kennedy died just a couple of months short of a 5-year 庚 Kyoung Metal luck cycle.)

Summary

The dynamics of the Heavenly Stems are important tools in saju interpretation and learners should be able to readily access the information.

The Sixth Conjuctions		
甲己	*Gahp-Ghee* merger yields	EARTH
乙庚	*Eul-Kyoung* merger yields	METAL
丙辛	*Byoung-Shin* merger yields	WATER
丁壬	*Jeong-Yim* merger yields	WOOD
戊癸	*Moo-Gyeh* merger yields	FIRE
The Seventh Oppositions		
甲庚	*Gahp-Kyoung* clash	
乙辛	*Eul-Shin* clash	
丙壬	*Byoung-Yim* clash	
丁癸	*Jeong-Gyeh* clash	

***

Chapter 12 Exercise

1. Do you find any harmonious mergers or clashing oppositions among the Stems in your chart?

2. Do you find any harmonious mergers or clashing oppositions between your Stems and the Stems of your significant other(s)? Are the mergers (or the clashes) happening in the same Pillars between the charts?

Chapter 13 Dynamics of the Earthly Branches

Until you make the unconscious conscious, it will direct your life and you will call it fate.

CG Jung

The Twelve Earthly Branches merge and clash in a more complex manner than the Ten Heavenly Stems do. They phase in and out with vigorous energy to make sure that the four seasons transpire smoothly throughout the year. Each Branch has its own agenda, and in the process of carrying out its mission, it finds harmony and conflict in multiple settings. There are Branch combinations—whether harmonious or conflicting—that will generate a great synergy to impact the life of the saju owner, and there are some that will exert minimal effect. All combinations traditionally recognized in the Four Pillars system are introduced in this chapter.

The Harmonious Combinations of the Branches

The harmonious combinations of the Branches come in three forms: 1) Seasonal or Directional Groups; 2) the Triads; and 3) the Six Harmonious Pairs.

The Seasonal/Directional Groups

- 寅卯辰 SPRING: 寅Inn and 卯 Myo Woods, together with 辰 Jin Earth, dominate the East. Their combined energy is Wood.
- 巳午未 SUMMER: 巳 Sah and 午Oh Fires, together with 未 Mee Earth, dominate the South. Their combined energy is Fire.

- 申酉戌 AUTUMN: 申 Shin and 酉 Yoo Metals, together with 戌 Sool Earth, dominate the West. Their combined energy is Metal.
- 亥子丑 WINTER: 亥 Hae and 子 Jah Waters, together with 丑 Chook Earth, dominate the North. Their combined energy is Water.

The first form of harmonious combination is based on the seasonal flow of the Twelve Branches in the order as they come. This is also called the directional combination. The energy of spring comes from the east, summer from the south, autumn from the west, and winter from the north. There are three Branches per group; each group has the yin and yang versions of one element, with a supportive Earth Branch attached at the end. Each group represents one season and yields one seasonal energy. As a result, the Earth Branch in each group relinquishes its elemental identity in support of the seasonal energy of the group.

When we take one Branch from each seasonal/directional group, we can recognize the following pattern:

1. The *first* Branch in each group is 寅巳申亥 (*Inn-Sah-Shin-Hae*); each stands for the *beginning* of a season. They represent Wood, Fire, Metal, and Water, respectively. As the leaders of their seasons, they possess yang energy. (巳 & 亥 are *interpreted* as yang Branches.) The four Branches individually carry the dynamics of "Traveling Horse" that are associated with active movement and distant travels. Finding one or more of these Branches in the saju chart translates to an active life involving extensive travel luck.

2. The *second* Branch in each group is 子卯午酉 (*Jah-Myo-Oh-Yoo*); each stands for the *middle* of a season. Occupying the middle ground, they are known as the kings of their seasons. They all possess yin energy. (子 & 午 are

interpreted as yin Branches.) These Branches carry the dynamics of "Peach Blossom" that are associated with physical (sexual) attractiveness, stubbornness, and purity.

3. The *third* Branch in each group is 辰未戌丑 (*Jin-Mee-Sool-Chook*); each stands for the *end* of a season. These are the four Earth Phase Branches that fill the transitional periods between seasons. The Earth Branches carry the dynamics of "Ornate Palanquin" that are associated with contemplation, religiosity, honor, reverence, and artistic talent.

The Harmonious Triads

- 亥卯未 WOOD: 亥 Hae Water, 卯 Myo Wood, and 未 Mee Earth
- 寅午戌 FIRE: 寅 Inn Wood, 午 Oh Fire, and 戌 Sool Earth
- 巳酉丑 METAL: 巳 Sah Fire, 酉 Yoo Metal, and 丑 Chook Earth
- 申子辰 WATER: 申 Shin Metal, 子 Jah Water, and 辰 Jin Earth

The Triads are a coalition of Branches taken from different seasonal groupings based on their mutual interest; and their mutual interest has to do with representing a single element that is associated with them in some ways. The 亥卯未 Triad, for instance, includes Water, Wood, and Earth Branches, but their combination yields one dominant energy of Wood, following the lead of 卯 Myo Wood in the center. The Hidden-Stems-in-Branches Table (Table 11.1) indicates 亥 Hae Water to be the birthplace of the Wood Phase, and 未 Mee Earth as its deathbed. Thus, the 亥卯未 Triad is associated with the life cycle of the Wood Phase, with its birthplace, kingship, and deathbed represented by the three Branches. Likewise, the 寅午戌 Triad is associated with the life cycle of the Fire Phase, with 寅 Inn Wood as its birthplace, 午 Oh Fire as the king, and 戌 Sool Earth as its deathbed. The 戌 Sool Earth is known as the Storage of Fire for this reason. The flickering fire energy hidden inside its middle period lies like a coffin inside a grave, and this imagery generates analytical implications. This scenario applies to all other Earth Branches that serve as storages.

In a Triad, the king always stands in the middle, and the associated Branches stand on the sides. When we take one Branch from each Triad, we can recognize the following pattern:

1. The *first* Branch in each Triad, 亥寅巳申 (*Hae-Inn-Sah-Shin*), makes up the four Branches representing Traveling Horse.

2. The *second* Branch in each Triad, 卯午酉子 (*Myo-Oh-Yoo-Jah*), makes up the four Branches representing Peach Blossom.

3. The *third* Branch from each Triad, 未戌丑辰 (*Mee-Sool-Chook-Jin*), makes up the four Earth Branches representing Ornate Palanquin.

When a Harmonious Triad is present in the saju composition, the analyst must recognize the presence of a single, unified energy—one that is greater than the sum of its parts. When a saju has only two Branches of a Triad, it is still considered to have a partial effect of a full Triad. When the missing Branch happens to come via the luck cycles and joins the "partial" Triad, the effect is then increased to 100 percent.

The Six Harmonious Pairs

1	2	3	4	5	6	7	8	9	10	11	12
yang water	yin earth	yang wood	yin wood	yang earth	yin fire	yang fire	yin earth	yang metal	yin metal	yang earth	yin water
子	丑	寅	卯	辰	巳	午	未	申	酉	戌	亥
jah	chook	inn	myo	jin	sah	oh	mee	shin	yoo	sool	hae

The Twelve Branches are numbered in the order of their natural sequence above. Each Branch pairs up harmoniously with just one other Branch, so the result is a total of six pairs. The harmonious pairs always comprise one odd numbered (yang) and one even numbered (yin) Branch.

1. 子丑 (1, 2) Jah Water and Chook Earth yields Water Earth
2. 寅亥 (3, 12) Inn Wood and Hae Water yields Wood
3. 卯戌 (4, 11) Myo Wood and Sool Earth yields Fire
4. 辰酉 (5, 10) Jin Earth and Yoo Metal yields Metal
5. 巳申 (6, 9) Sah Fire and Shin Metal yields Water
6. 午未 (7, 8) Oh Fire and Mee Earth yields Fire Earth

Each pair yields one of the Five Elements that flows in the direction of the four seasons. From 子丑's watery earth comes the Wood of spring achieved by the 寅亥 pair that nurtures the Fire energy of 卯戌 of summer, which is then transformed into the 辰酉's Metal energy of autumn, then finally moving onto the 巳申's Water energy of winter.

The 午未 pair stands on the opposite end of the first pair, 子丑. Due to their difference in elements as fire and water, the 午未 pair (hot, bright earth) is symbolized as the sun, and the 子丑 pair (cold, dark earth) is symbolized as the moon. The movements of the sun, moon, and the earth together sustain the time-space continuum manifested in the four seasons of the year.

The figure above illustrates the Twelve Branches lined up in a circular, clockwise direction around the globe. Each Branch is facing its harmonious counterpart directly across the globe as a result. The harmonious pairs are linked by a horizontal line indicating the type of energy they procreate. The tilted globe is a depiction of the earth's axial tilt at 23.4 degrees that allows for the actualization of the four seasons as we know it.

About the Inauspicious Branch Combinations

There are numerous inauspicious combinations of the Twelve Earthly Branches—more so than there are harmonious mergers—that appear in the ancient texts of Four Pillars philosophy. It is unnecessary to go through all of them, especially when they don't seem to have any practical value in the present times. The inauspicious Branch combinations exist to provide a type of warning, so that the person can mind her luck, and be careful when she needs to exercise extra caution. At the same time, however, the emphasis on the individual luck has become a debatable point in our postmodern era. We live in a highly globalized, interdependent world, and with the exponential increase in population since antiquity, human communities of all kinds and sizes share compact living spaces where one's destiny can hardly be influenced by individual luck alone. We live in high-rises with multitudes of tenants, drive on roads shared by a countless number of vehicles, fly on planes with hundreds of other passengers, and live in an age of global warming, weapons of mass destruction, wars, pandemics, and monstrous cyclones, where butterfly effects occurring across the global village are increasingly becoming a worrisome reality. Sometimes, what happens to us goes beyond our individual luck, especially when we find ourselves in the throes of natural and man-made disasters.

Nevertheless, we are the vessels of our individual destiny. We have our personal, relational, and social spheres to tend to, and we desire to improve our experiences in all of these areas. There are four Branches in our saju chart (and more Branches in the luck cycles) that we must heed in our pursuit of our well-being; and we need to watch out for the ones that come in our way in the form of inauspicious Branch combinations.

The Conflicting Combinations of the Branches

The conflicting combinations of the Branches come in five forms: 1) the Six Clashing Pairs; 2) the Penal Triads/Duos; 3) the Disruptors; 4) the Interrupters; and 5) the Antagonizers. The clashing pairs, Penal Triads, and the antagonizers are the ones I pay most attention to when interpreting a saju chart. These combinations tend to generate significant and visible effects on people's lives. The disruptors and the interrupters are a little complicated to work with, because they include Branch pairs that can be found in other categories under both harmonious and conflicting combinations. So, there is some overlap. Such complexity is based on the chemistry between the Branches as natural elements, and also on the workings of the Hidden-Stems in the Branches.

The Six Pairs of Clashing Branches

The Twelve Earthly Branches come with six pairs of clashing combinations. Each combination is made up of two Branches of conflicting elements that have the same yin-yang energy.
1. 子午 yang water clashes with yang fire (water vs. fire)
2. 丑未 yin earth clashes with yin earth (metal earth vs. wood earth)
3. 寅申 yang wood clashes with yang metal (wood vs. metal)
4. 卯酉 yin wood clashes with yin metal (wood vs. metal)

5. 辰戌 yang earth clashes with yang earth (water earth vs. fire earth)
6. 巳亥 yin fire clashes with yin water (water vs. fire)

The clashing combinations of water vs. fire and metal vs. wood appear to be self-explanatory, but the clashes between the Earth Branches require an examination. To understand, we need to recall the *storage* function of the Earth Branches. At the end of every season, the four Earth Branches store up their previous season's energies—wood (未), fire (戌), metal (丑), and water (辰). Hence, when the Earth Branches are paired up, their clash is occurring inside the earth. The 丑未 clash is about Metal and Wood clashing inside the earth; and the 辰戌 clash is about Water and Fire clashing inside the earth.

The dynamics of the Earth Phase Branches require special attention in saju analysis. The 丑未 Chook-Mee clash and the 辰戌 Jin-Sool clash may not immediately raise red flags as other, more obvious, clashing combinations may. The disharmony arising from these clashing pairs may seem hidden, and may take time to come out in the open. This, however, does not minimize their clashing effect when the conflict is revealed. Consider earthquakes and active volcanoes; the earth remains quiet until it is ready to make noise.

The Penal Triads and Penal Duos

The Penal Triads represent groups of Branches that have conflicting agendas, and so the Branches don't mingle well together as a group. The intensity of the discord is most powerful when all three Branches are present, and the cumulated energy can yield serious and/or unfavorable circumstances in the life of the saju owner. The significance of the Penal Triads is discussed further in the next section.

The Penal Duos are composed of two of the same Branch, except for the 子卯 Jah-Myo combination. The term "penal" is associated with punishment, hardship or difficulty, and this is the effect the Penal Duos exert on people on psychological and emotional levels. This is due to the conflicting characteristics a Branch possesses within itself, and when the same Branch is added, the conflictual state is augmented. For instance, 亥 Hae Water is endowed with the conflicting impulses to condense (as a water element) and to expand (as the leader of a new season), and thus, it is prone to experiencing difficulty in making decisions. When another 亥 Hae Water is combined to make a Penal Duo, the difficulty becomes multiplied. The 子卯 Jah-Myo Penal Duo has a different story of conflict: the 卯 Myo Wood longs for the nurturing support of 子 Jah Water, but it won't give it, because 子 Jah Water has to stay true to its self-isolating nature.

- The Penal Triads: 寅巳申 and 丑戌未
- The Penal Duos: 亥亥, 辰辰, 午午, 酉酉, and 子卯

The Disruptors
The disruptors come in pairs of Branches that represent different seasons. Their differences translate to different agendas causing disruptions in each other's paths, but their effect is not as significant as other conflicting combinations. The pairs need to stand next to each other to produce their disrupting effect in the saju chart.

- 辰丑, 辰未, 巳申, 亥寅, 酉子, 卯午

The Interrupters
The interrupters are probably the least harmful pairs, but they can still exert influence in people's lives. The first two on the list—子未 and 丑午—are also listed under the antagonizers, so they should not all be dismissed as being benign.

- 子未, 丑午, 寅巳, 辰卯, 申亥, 酉戌

The Antagonizers

The Antagonizers come in pairs that don't get along well because of their hindering relationship. For instance, 辰 Jin Earth prevents Water from staying active by locking it up throughout the summer months; it fulfills this role as the Storage of Water (the deathbed of Water). Hence, 亥 Hae Water's role is hindered during the months ensuing 辰 Jin Earth, which creates an air of animosity between 亥 Hae Water and 辰 Jin Earth. When a pair of antagonizers stand next to each other in the saju chart, the saju owner may be prone to encountering situations of distress related to relationships, work, study, and finances, depending on which archetypes the antagonizers represent to the Day Master and where they are located in the chart. The effect of the antagonizers tends to be psychological and emotional in nature, but it could also involve tricking the mind, causing the saju owner to do things out of character and cause trouble. If the antagonizers are formed by the Branches coming from the luck cycles, the effect lasts for the duration of the luck cycles.

- 子未, 丑午, 寅酉, 卯申, 辰亥, 巳戌

The Branches as the *Shin-Sahl* Generators

There are Branch combinations that are known as *shin-sahl*, which is a term that originates from the two Han characters—神 煞. 神 (*shin*) means god, or spirit; 煞 (*sahl*) means curse, or killing energy. *Shin-sahl* can thus be translated as "god and curse," or "auspicious and inauspicious luck." In interpretative usage, a "god" refers to a benevolent force that supports and protects the saju owner; and a "curse" refers to a negative or harmful force that enters the life of the saju owner to cause an upheaval in varying degrees.

There are hundreds of *shin-sahls* that have been named since ancient times, but their theoretical origins, for the most part, are unclear, and their applicability in saju interpretation has been under much debate. There are saju scholars who dismiss the utility of *shin-sahls* entirely, and there are those who treat *shin-sahls* as the primary tool for interpretation. I believe that an average saju reader would take note of the presence of different *shin-sahls* in the saju and diagnose the life of the querent with their effects in mind. Sometimes, a *shin-sahl* has little or no effect; other times, it can wield a powerful effect on the querent's life. Identifying a dormant or an active *shin-sahl* is not so easy, since times are moving and changing constantly. A dormant *shin-sahl* could awaken and cause an effect if the right set of Branches show up in the luck cycles, or if the querent becomes involved with a significant other whose saju comes with the right components to activate the querent's *shin-sahl*. (This is why relationships with other people play an important role in shaping one's destiny.)

Generally, *shin-sahls* are met with negativity because the term ends with the word "curse." But not all *shin-sahls* cause trouble and harm. There are *shin-sahls* that bring good luck and yield positive effects; this is the work of the "helpful gods" in our lives. *Shin-sahls* that fend off evil and protect the saju owner are like the guardian angels, and their presence can be much appreciated. Some *shin-sahls* are neutral, as they can be either advantageous or disadvantageous. *Shin-sahls* such as Traveling Horse, Peach Blossom, and Ornate Palanquin mentioned in this chapter are considered to be neutral; they have either positive or negative effects, depending on one's saju composition. The concept of *gongmang* that was introduced in Chapter 8 is also a type of *shin-sahl*, and its effect can go either way, depending on the circumstances facing the saju owner in the timeframe affected by the *gongmang* Branches.

Different Types of *Shin-Sahls*

Discussing the *shin-sahls* can take up the space of a whole book, so I have listed just a few of the important ones used in saju interpretation.

Traveling Horse

Branches 寅, 申, 巳, 亥 (Inn, Shin, Sah, Hae) comprise the Traveling Horse *shin-sahl* that is associated with active movement and distant travels. 巳 Sah Fire and 亥 Hae Water in particular represent overseas travel. If these Branches are found in the Day Pillar, the effect is most significant; the effect is diminished in other Pillars—in the order of Month, Hour, and Year Pillars. The Traveling Horse found in the Year Pillar has the least influence, unless another Traveling Horse is found in the saju in which case the whole effect is increased substantially. When the Traveling Horse is found in the luck cycle(s), it often translates to voluntary or involuntary travel engagements occurring in the life of the querent for the time period defined by the luck cycle. 寅 Inn Wood and 申 Shin Metal are usually associated with domestic travel, and when they show up *together* as a clashing pair, the traveler should beware of accidents related to travel.

Peach Blossom

Branches 子, 卯, 午, 酉 (Jah, Myo, Oh, Yoo) comprise the Peach Blossom *shin-sahl* that is associated with personal attractiveness through appearance and/or personality. The Day Pillar Peach Blossom wields the most influence, followed by the Month and Hour Pillars. The Year Pillar Peach Blossom tends to have little effect on the saju owner but it is possible to interpret that the effect lies with one's ancestors. People with high-powered Peach Blossom are likely to be socialites with attractive appearances. Entertainers are often equipped with this *shin-sahl*. Even if a Peach Blossom is not found in one's Four Pillars, it can come as a Larger Luck cycle, generating just as strong an effect for that time frame. The downside of this *shin-sahl* includes difficulty with maintaining intimate relationships; if one is too outgoing and overly popular, one's partner may sustain jealousy or anxiety over the fear of losing him or her.

Ornate Palanquin

The four Earth Branches 辰, 未, 戌, 丑 (Jin, Mee, Sool, Chook) comprise the Ornate Palanquin *shin-sahl* that is associated with the practice of prayer and contemplation, and the status of honor and reverence. In the olden days, the beautifully decorated litters were used by people of high-status including royalty and nobility, and perhaps also by brides on their wedding day. As a human-powered transport, a palanquin is an enclosed space for usually just one person. Ornate Palanquin is associated with glory and honor, but also with solitary existence, which is linked to religion and a hermetic life involving spiritual practice or artistry.

Gongmang

Gongmang refers to "empty" and "ruin" in Han characters. Every saju comes with a pair of *gongmang* Branches. (See Appendix B to find your *gongmang* pair.) This is two consecutive Branches out of the twelve, so every saju owner will face 2 *gongmang* years after every 10 years. *Gongmang* years are like the weekend after a busy week of hard work; it is meant to be a time of renewal, so starting something big or risky is not advised during one's *gongmang* years. The *gongmang* years don't affect all saju owners equally. For some, they hardly feel anything before the 2 years pass; for others, they experience the most challenging years of their life. If one's *gongmang* Branch is found within the saju composition, the Stem sitting above it can be affected, as in losing its effectiveness as an element or an archetype. Importantly, a *gongmang* Branch *can* lose its *gongmang* effect if it happens to merge or clash with other Branch(es) in the saju or with an incoming Branch from the luck cycle.

Penal Triad

Penal Triad is a *shin-sahl* that can have negative effects in the life of the saju owner, especially if all three Branches are found in the saju composition. The effects include suffering in the areas of psychological, physical, social, and monetary hardship, which is viewed as a type of karmic judgment placed on the Self. There are two sets of Penal Triad: 1) 寅巳申 (Inn-Sah-Shin); 2) 丑戌未 (Chook-Sool-Mee). It may be rare to find all three Branches of a Penal Triad in a saju chart, but having just two out of three Branches still makes a "partial" Penal Triad, since the third missing Branch will most definitely show up in the luck cycles over time. The 寅巳申 (Inn-Sah-Shin) Penal Triad is known to stimulate the Self with extraordinary energy and strength to do good or harm, depending on what is on one's mind. The focus is on the Self; thus, the saju owner should be aware of oneself and not be controlled by anger or greed to avoid trouble. The 丑戌未 (Chook-Sool-Mee) Penal Triad tends to affect the saju owner with psychological instability, causing unstable relationship patterns, mismanagement of money, health issues, or a profound desire to pursue a religious path to find peace and stability. The danger of a betrayal—in regards to money or relationship or both—is also associated with the 丑戌未 Penal Triad.

The Nobleman*

This is the most beneficial *shin-sahl* there is. There are several kinds of Noblemen and the best one of all is the Nobleman of Heavens. The Nobleman of Heavens is the divine helper who can bring you blessings and protect you from harm. It can help you to see the opportunity in a crisis situation and help you to follow through. You can find your Nobleman of Heavens by referencing the chart below. (*Nobleman is used here as a gender-neutral term.)

Day Master	甲, 戊, 庚	乙, 己	丙, 丁	辛	壬, 癸
Nobleman of Heavens	丑, 未	申, 子	亥, 酉	寅, 午	卯, 巳

Every Day Master is given two Nobleman of Heavens represented by two Branches. (辰 Jin Earth and 戌 Sool Earth are not included in the chart, as they are used in other power wielding *shin-sahls*.) The Nobleman of Heavens found in the Day Pillar exert the most influence, followed by the ones found in the Month, Hour, and Year Pillar. It is important not to clash with your Nobleman, in which case the effect may not only be less positive but actually be negative. A Nobleman that is one of your *gongmang* Branches can be helpless rather than helpful. In general, if a Nobleman of Heavens is found in your chart or comes via the luck cycles, you may encounter unexpected help from others that can significantly alter the quality of your life for the better. If your significant other has a saju containing your Nobleman of Heavens, he or she can be a help-giving person in your life. Keeping an attitude of humility and gratitude can augment the good fortune brought forth by the Nobleman of Heavens.

Heaven's Gate Star

Two or more combinations of the following Branches form the Heaven's Gate Star: 未, 戌, 卯, 亥, 寅, 酉. Among the six, 戌 Sool Earth and 亥 Hae Water are the most influential, and unlike the others, these two Branches can stand alone to extend their effect. People with Heaven's Gate Star, especially if the Branches reside in their Day or Month Pillar, are spiritually open individuals who seek after otherworldly knowledge—in religion, medicine, astronomy, or astrology. They can show competency as saju readers as well. Characteristics of the Heaven's Gate Star include well-developed intuition, awareness, and sensitivity that lead to interests in the transcendental reality, particularly in the areas of spirituality, literature, and religion. Even if the Heaven's Gate Star is not found in the saju, it can show up in the incoming luck cycles that translate to a time frame one can devote to cultivating one's spirituality.

Summary

The dynamics of the Earthly Branches are important tools in saju interpretation, and learners should be able to readily access the information.

Harmonious Branch Combinations		
Directional/Seasonal	**The Triads**	**The Six Pairs**
寅卯辰 EAST•Wood	亥卯未 WOOD	子丑 Water Earth
巳午未 SOUTH•Fire	寅午戌 FIRE	寅亥 Wood
申酉戌 WEST•Metal	巳酉丑 METAL	卯戌 Fire
亥子丑 NORTH•Water	申子辰 WATER	辰酉 Metal
		巳申 Water
		午未 Fire Earth

Conflicting Branch Combinations				
Six Clashing Pairs	**Penal Triads/Duos**	**Disruptors**	**Interrupters**	**Antagonizers**
子午	寅巳申	辰丑	子未	子未
丑未	丑戌未	辰未	丑午	丑午
寅申	亥亥	巳申	寅巳	寅酉
卯酉	辰辰	亥寅	辰卯	卯申
辰戌	午午	酉子	申亥	辰亥
巳亥	酉酉	卯午	酉戌	巳戌
	子卯			

***

Chapter 13 Exercise

1. Do you find any harmonious mergers or clashing oppositions among the Branches in your chart?
2. Do you find any harmonious mergers or clashing oppositions between your Branches and the Branches of your significant other(s)?
3. Find the Nobleman of Heavens for your Day Master.

Chapter 14 The Ten Archetypes

The good life is one inspired by love and guided by knowledge.
Bertrand Russell

The Ten Archetypes are established based on the relationships among the Five Elements, and they serve as one of the primary tools for saju analysis. Seventy to eighty percent of saju interpretation can be accomplished by using the Ten Archetypes theory. Your knowledge of the Five Elements and their relational dynamics will be useful in comprehending the different archetypes.

In analysis, the archetypes are determined by the elemental relationship between the Day Master and the rest of the characters occupying the Four Pillars. From the Day Master's standpoint, a Stem or a Branch can be nurturing, controlling, rivaling, or requiring the Day Master's nurture or control. All relationships boil down to these five, based on the relational dynamics of the Five Elements seen on the human scale. In technical terms, the Five Relationships are: Rivalry, Output, Wealth, Power, and Resource.

***

♦In the original texts on Four Pillars philosophy, the Ten Archetypes are called the "Ten Gods" or the "Ten Stars." They are also called the "Six Relationships," referring to the intimate relationships via consanguinity or marriage.

***

The Five Relationships

The Ten Archetypes are derived from the following Five Relationships. These constitute the intimate relationships in the categories of parents, siblings, spouses (wife and husband), and children.

Rivalry

Rivalry shares the same element with the Day Master. It tries to act and be like the Self, so it generates a spirit of competition in the saju layout. In analysis, Rivalry stands for siblings, friends, colleagues, and competitors. It can also be interpreted as another version of the Self.

Output

Output represents the element nurtured by the Day Master. It reveals the creative and the expressive side of the Self, keeping the Self to stay busy with work. In analysis, Output stands for talent, work, job, skill, craft, and children in female charts.

Wealth

Wealth represents the element controlled by the Self. Like Output, it also seeks the attention and the energy of the Self in the saju layout. In analysis, Wealth stands for money, father, and wife in male charts.

Power

Power represents the element controlling the Self. This is the most challenging, or the most enervating, relationship the Self can have with another Stem or a Branch. In analysis, Power stands for work, career, rank, husband in female charts, and children in male charts.

Resource

Resource represents the element nurturing the Self. This is the most helpful relationship the Self can have with another Stem or a Branch. In analysis, Resource stands for mother, education, certification, contract, degree, religion, teacher, and spiritual leader.

The Ten Archetypes

The Five Relationships yield the Ten Archetypes when each relationship is divided into two subcategories according to the yin-yang energy of the element.

The Ten Archetypes		
Rivalry	The Sibling	Yin-yang energy is same as the Self.
	The Stealer of Wealth	Yin-yang energy is different from the Self.
Output	The Eating God	Yin-yang energy is same as the Self.
	The Injurer of Controller	Yin-yang energy is different from the Self.
Wealth	Indirect Wealth	Yin-yang energy is same as the Self.
	Proper Wealth	Yin-yang energy is different from the Self.
Power	Indirect Power	Yin-yang energy is same as the Self.
	Proper Power	Yin-yang energy is different from the Self.
Resource	Indirect Resource	Yin-yang energy is same as the Self.
	Proper Resource	Yin-yang energy is different from the Self.

Rivalry

Archetype 1: The Sibling

The Sibling comes in the category of Rivalry and shares the same element and the same yin-yang energy with the Day Master. The Sibling is the splitting image of the Self, equipped with equal power and identical nature. In saju analysis, the Sibling can represent one's actual sibling(s) or person(s) close to the Self in age, including peers, cousins, colleagues, business partners, and competitors. The Sibling naturally augments the strength of the Day Master, which translates to a strong sense of independence, pride, self-esteem, and inflated ego. This is especially the case when a Sibling is found in the same pillar with the Day Master. Never underestimate the strength—both physical and mental—of individuals whose Day Pillars are made up of one solid element with the presence of a Sibling in the Day Branch.

People with several Siblings in their saju tend to be strong willed, competitive in spirit, stubborn, opinionated, and less social. They enjoy the attention of others (sometimes falsely assuming they are entitled to it), but they dislike the rules and control imposed by others. Endowed with a drive and ambition, they can be high achievers given the extra support and strength contributed by the Siblings in the saju composition.

An example of a saju with several Siblings is Stephen Hawking's chart that was introduced in Chapter 3.

Hour	Day	Month	Year
癸	辛	辛	辛
eul	shin	shin	shin
yin wood	yin metal	yin metal	yin metal
巳	酉	丑	巳
sah	yoo	chook	sah
yin fire	yin metal	yin earth	yin fire

Hawking's chart indicates several Siblings where the Year and the Month Pillars have the exact same Stem as the Day Master.

Moreover, the Branches in the Year, Month, Day, and Hour Pillars create the harmonious combination of the 巳酉丑 Triad (not just once, but twice, given the presence of two 巳 Sah Fires), resulting in a powerful yin metal energy, which even further strengthens the 辛 Shin Metal Day Master. (In this case, the 丑 Chook Earth and the 巳 Sah Fires give up their elemental identity and follow the 酉 Yoo Metal's lead to produce Metal.) We can thus say that all Four Pillars (excluding the Hour Stem) are comprised of Siblings. The combination of these seven Stems and Branches happens to create one unified energy of yin Metal—the kind that is already tamed by fire and is ready to serve a specific purpose. The prolific presence of yin Metal in the saju can be translated as Hawking's sheer will power and driving force to succeed against all odds. Hawking had made his environment conform to him and not the other way around. He'd lived a reclusive life not only because of his illness, but also as a thinker unlike others, pushing the limits of scientific knowledge from his private world of research.

Archetype 2: The Stealer of Wealth

The Stealer of Wealth shares the same element with the Day Master but it comes in different yin-yang energy. If you (Self) are a yang wood, your Stealer of Wealth is a yin wood; if you are a yin fire, your Stealer of Wealth is a yang fire, and so on. The Stealer of Wealth is still a rival to the Day Master like the Sibling, but it is given this strange title of "stealer of wealth," because the element representing this archetype is the direct opponent (controller) of the Day Master's Wealth element. As a structural rule, this is the case in all saju charts. The concept is similar to this scenario: Someone is about to hand you a hundred-dollar bill but your brother violently pushes the person away. Your brother is considered the Stealer of Wealth, because he prevented you from acquiring the money.

Being the same element, the Stealer of Wealth *can* increase the strength of the Day Master, especially if the Day Master is considered to be weak within the saju composition. However, too much untamable force in the form of the Stealer of Wealth is undesirable. People with several Stealers of Wealth in their saju are free thinkers, unafraid of competition, and willing to take from others. They don't seem to be bound by societal rules or norms, but tend to be the pioneers of their own worlds. Their driving force is unique to themselves, so they do better as lone wolves than to go against their instinct in trying to cooperate with and please others. Naturally, they can be difficult people as teammates or business partners. In the saju chart, it is a good thing to find a Proper Power near a Stealer of Wealth in order to tame its overconfident disposition that may lead to relationship issues or financial problems.

Output

Archetype 3: The Eating God

The Eating God is an element nurtured by the Day Master and has the same yin-yang energy. If the Self is a yang water, the Eating God is a yang wood. If the Self is a yin fire, the Eating God is a yin earth. The Eating God is placed in the Output category because it puts the Day Master to work. The act of nurturing (output) by the Day Master translates to income security (food security in the olden days, hence the term "Eating God"), financial affluence, and offspring for women. The Eating God keeps the Self to stay busy and active, encouraging productivity. It can also symbolize creativity, talent, skills, ideas, and expression—especially through the vocal means using the mouth.

Too much Output in the form of the Eating God is not desirable since the effect can be just the opposite—

counterproductive. (Remember that when the yang energy reaches its height, the yin begins to develop and expand; too much of one thing can be equal to having none of it.) Multiple Outputs can also enervate the Day Master from too much work, potentially leading to workaholism or perfectionism in regards to work habits. People with Eating Gods in their prime Pillars tend to be optimistic and enjoy being entertained. They can also be excellent entertainers or teachers themselves, given their vocal skills.

Archetype 4: The Injurer of Controller

The Injurer of Controller is an element nurtured by the Day Master but has the different yin-yang energy. As an Output, it is a productivity god just like the Eating God, but because of the yin-yang harmony it achieves with the Day Master, its effects are more dynamic, creative, noticeable, and even flamboyant. It is given its name because the element representing Injurer of Controller directly challenges the element representing Proper Power, a controller to the Self. This is a structural rule and applies to all saju charts.

The ability to challenge the Proper Power translates to resistance to authority, insubordination to rules and regulations, advocacy of justice, ingenious creativity, artistic brilliance, talents in entertainment, and highly developed speech. People with Injurer of Controller in their prime Pillars (as in Day or Month Pillar) love to speak—with fluency—and receive attention, and they are likely to choose career paths that allow them to express themselves through the mouth. They include teachers, entertainers (e.g., actors, singers), news anchors, reporters, motivation speakers, consultants, and trainers.

An example of a saju with well-developed Output in both versions of Eating God and Injurer of Controller is Michael Jackson's chart that was introduced in Chapter 2.

Hour	Day	Month	Year
辛	戊	庚	戊
shin yin metal	*moo* yang earth	*kyoung* yang metal	*moo* yang earth
酉	寅	申	戌
yoo yin metal	*moo* yang wood	*shin* yang metal	*sool* yang earth

In Jackson's chart, the entire Year Pillar is occupied by two Siblings, adding substantial strength to the 戊 Moo Earth Day Master. Jackson does come from a large family as he was the eighth among ten children, so he had many siblings in real life. He started his singing career early on; he was only 6 years old when he debuted with his older brothers. Work had always been a significant part of his life since childhood—practicing his craft in private and performing with passion and charisma in public. He passed away at the young age of 50, but his legacy of 4 decades of superstardom continues to this day, influencing entertainment industries around the world.

In the chart, there are two well-developed (meaning that a Pillar is wholly occupied by a single element) Output Pillars—the Eating Gods in the entire Month Pillar and the Injurers of Controller in the entire Hour Pillar. Further, the three Branches, 申酉戌, create the harmonious seasonal/directional combination to yield more Metal; so, the owner of this saju actually loses the 戌 Sool Earth and gains a Metal in its place, adding to the number of Outputs in the chart. Now, you can imagine the precarious position of 寅 Inn Wood in the Day Pillar that is surrounded by not four but five Metals constantly threatening its well-being. The 寅 Inn Wood, in the case of Jackson's saju, serves a critical role in maintaining the Day Master's health and intimate relationships. Jackson suffered from a number of illnesses including a skin disease, and was concerned for his health to the point of being called a "health fanatic." Factual details aside, it appears to be the strain of overwork that had consumed the life of the singer.

Wealth

Archetype 5: The Indirect Wealth

The Indirect Wealth is an element controlled by the Day Master and has the same yin-yang energy. The term "indirect" is used here to describe something that is one-sided, partial, or unbalanced, thus generating a sense of instability and/or riskiness. As such, the Indirect Wealth can represent extreme wealth or no wealth, depending on the saju composition and the incoming luck cycles.

When the Day Master is in the position to control an element, the element represents wealth, money, and asset to the Self. For male charts, the Wealth category is traditionally interpreted as both money and woman. So, a man with several Indirect or Proper Wealths in his chart is likely to have a good amount of money and women passing through in life. (The question is whether he can continue to possess money and women, since having too much of something can equal having none.)

Some saju consultants with feminist inclinations argue against interpreting Wealth as woman for male charts because of the "controlling" nature of the relationship. I believe one should employ flexibility, and it is okay to ask the querent and verify the circumstances rather than to make analytical assumptions that may be incorrect or out of context. Meanwhile, the tendency of rich men to easily attract women has not changed all that much today. So, the traditional interpretation still applies. For female charts, the Wealth category is generally interpreted as money and also "father," according to the traditional notion that a father is usually the financial provider in the family.

The Indirect Wealth, by sharing the same yin-yang energy with the Self, makes its influence less obvious. There is an air of unpredictability and cavalier sentiment associated with it. With an Indirect Wealth nearby, the Day Master can be tempted to invest or gamble, and not mind taking risks and may even enjoy the adventure. This is a different mentality from accepting hard work to earn money. In the olden days, an Indirect Wealth represented a female lover or a mistress as opposed to a legally married wife for male charts. This interpretation appears obsolete today; the entire Wealth category should be seen as "significant other" for men including a wife.

For both male and female charts, the Indirect Wealth also symbolizes a windfall (or unexpected financial loss) depending on the saju composition. In a saju where the Day Master is positioned with strength, an Indirect Wealth *can* translate to a substantial financial success. The key word is *strength*; the Day Master must have the adequate power to control Wealth. A weak Self facing several Wealths—either Indirect or Proper—is not desirable, and it can even be harmful. We must recall the rules of relationships that apply to the Five Phases noted in Chapter 5: "The controller can be *harmed* by the stronger counterpart."

An example of a saju with several Indirect Wealths is Princess Diana's chart that was introduced in Chapter 3.

Hour	Day	Month	Year
癸	乙	甲	辛
gyeh yin water	*eul* yin wood	*gahp* yang wood	*shin* yin metal
未	未	午	丑
mee yin earth	*mee* yin earth	*oh* yang fire	*chook* yin earth

156

Except for the Month Branch, the entire bottom row is occupied by Indirect Wealths represented by one 丑 Chook Earth and two 未 Mee Earths. This is a strong presence of Indirect Wealths, which is further strengthened by the 午 Oh Fire in the Month Branch. (Fire nurtures Earth.) From birth to death, Princess Diana never experienced a lack of wealth, though it isn't exactly the kind of wealth earned by one's hard labor, which is in line with the nature of Indirect Wealths. Marrying into the British royal family at a young age can be interpreted as a windfall as well.

As a member of the royalty, the princess had led a public life in glamor and popularity in light of her 乙 Eul Wood Day Master that exudes warmth, kindness, friendliness, and attractiveness. The 甲 Gahp Wood in the Month Pillar, while protecting the Day Master from the 辛 Shin Metal in the Year Pillar (i.e. 乙 辛 clash), is contributing toward her leadership, inspirational presence, compassion, and benevolence evidenced in her work of activism and charity. But, even with the support of 甲 Gahp Wood and 癸 Gyeh Water, the 乙 Eul Wood is being enervated, having to relentlessly tame—throughout her life—the scorched Earths of Indirect Wealths. Despite her (family) fortunes, her private life was full of upheaval, ending in a highly publicized divorce followed by a deadly car crash. She died during the Larger Luck cycle of 戊 Moo Earth (another Wealth Stem) in the year of 丁丑 that brought yet another Indirect Wealth into her saju composition. The relations rule #3, "The controller can be harmed by the stronger counterpart," utterly applies in the case of Princess Diana.

Archetype 6: The Proper Wealth

The Proper Wealth is an element controlled by the Day Master and has the different yin-yang energy. The yin-yang harmony between a Proper Wealth and the Day Master heightens the rational and practical nature of this archetype. The thought of "balance" is always on the mind of Proper Wealths. This is Wealth in the proper form, such as money gained through one's labor, and wealth accumulated by proper or traditional means. For male charts, it represents the wife proper. The Proper Wealth likes to play by the book; it values honor, reputation, trust, transparency, predictability, frugality, and plans for the future through a meticulous measure for accumulating wealth. The Proper Wealth doesn't take risks like the Indirect Wealth does. Its conservative nature can be criticized as being stingy, but its attitude toward wealth is considered healthier.

Power

Archetype 7: The Indirect Power

The Indirect Power is an element controlling the Day Master and has the same yin-yang energy. This is the *most challenging* relationship to the Self out of the Ten Archetypes because it is a controlling agent in the absence of the yin-yang harmony, which can be a serious source of distress and instability to the Day Master. The Power characters in general symbolize a "government post" or a high status in the work setting such as a CEO position. They can also represent offspring in male charts, and a male lover or a husband in female charts. The Indirect Power is associated with power, authority, decisiveness, ferocity, impatience, solitude, and suffering.

The effect of Indirect Powers is dependent on the saju composition. If the Day Master is poised with strength, meaning that there is a healthy balance between supportive and enervating elements in the chart, a nearby Indirect Power can help to achieve a high status with one's career. If the Day Master is weak, the influence tends to be negative, and can even be fatal if there is no nearby support to the Self. (Recall the rule #4 from Chapter 5: "The weak should fear encountering the controller.") People with strong Indirect Powers in their chart are likely to pursue careers associated with organized power or authority, including positions in politics, corporations, military, and government. Politicians, police officers, prosecutors, and lawyers commonly have Power archetypes in their charts. Jobs that require working with sharp tools also make the list—e.g., surgeons, nurses, hair stylists, culinary artists, etc. For female charts, Indirect Powers represent intimate relationships (with men), thus having too many can lead to multiple relationships or marriages in a lifetime; a remedy to avoid this is to find work that requires one to be surrounded by men. For both men and women, having several Indirect Powers near the Day Master can be a source of suffering, resulting in a sensitive, anxious temperament.

Archetype 8: The Proper Power

The Proper Power is an element controlling the Day Master and has the different yin-yang energy. Achieving the yin-yang harmony with the Self, the Proper Power seeks balance, stability, credibility, honor, and compassion. Its conservative nature keeps the Day Master in the proper path—law-abiding, virtuous, disciplined, and devoid of frivolity. The Proper Power does not seek to be the leader like the Indirect Power does, because being a leader has its ups and downs, but the Proper Power prefers stability and long-term commitments. There is a saying that the best employees are the people with just one Proper Power in their saju chart (without an Injurer of Controller nearby), as they will be loyal to their employer, follow the rules, and exhibit honorable manners.

For female charts, the Proper Power symbolizes the husband. Having just one Proper Power that doesn't clash or merge with other characters in the chart is considered to be the desirable case. While having too many can turn out to be not having any at all, multiple Proper Powers can result in multiple relationships or marriages. Again, a solution for female charts with multiple Power characters includes choosing an occupation that involves working with men. As a controlling force, the Indirect or the Proper Power can harm the Self if the forces increase to a dangerous level via the incoming luck cycles.

An example of a saju with several Power characters is J. F. Kennedy's chart that was introduced in Chapter 10.

The Year Pillar is wholly comprised of Fire, with an Indirect Power of 丁 Jeong Fire as Stem and a Proper Power of 巳 Sah Fire as Branch. (巳 Sah Fire is interpreted as yang in energy.) There is another 巳 Sah Fire in the Month Branch, which helps to create a powerful presence of Power in the saju composition. When Indirect and Proper Powers share a single Pillar or are situated next to or diagonally to each other, it is called the "Congested Powers" that describe a mixture of influences (usually negative) of Power on the Self. In the case of such a mixture, Proper Powers end up behaving like Indirect Powers.

As Power in general is associated with political and social ranks (especially for men's charts), J. F. Kennedy came from a family well-established in politics, and he himself pursued a political career early on. In the chart, the 辛 Shin Metal Day Master is surrounded by 乙 Eul Woods on both sides, representing family money in the form of Indirect Wealths, and also women, in the case of Kennedy as a male. The Day Master is considered extremely weak in this chart, due to the presence of several controllers (Powers) and the two Wealth Stems (乙) that are apparently clashing with the Day Master from both sides. There is really no breathing space for the Self in this kind of environment. Kennedy suffered from multiple illnesses growing up and also as an adult, and his health problems continued throughout his presidency. Perhaps we ought to place hope in the two Indirect Resources — 未 Mee Earths — that are giving some support to the 辛 Shin Metal Day Master. However, the problem with 未 Mee Earths is that 丁 乙己 Stems are hidden inside them, making them two fiery Earths that are unable to help the 辛 Day Master adequately. The Day Master certainly does not need more control from Power elements (丁) nor more Indirect Wealths (乙) to clash with. In the case of Kennedy, therefore, his Day Master is highly dependent on his Larger Luck cycles to find support and strength.

Resource

Archetype 9: The Indirect Resource

The Indirect Resource is an element nurturing the Day Master and has the same yin-yang energy. For both male and female charts, the Resource category symbolizes the "mother." In addition to Rivalry, Resource is a category that can augment the energy of the Day Master through its nurturing activity. It doesn't exhaust the Self like the Output, Wealth, and Power categories do. Resource offers a breathing space for the Self. The nurturing energy of Resource thus allows the Day Master to take the time to think and plan. This is the reason for its association with education, religion, art, and spirituality; one has to have the time and the space to study and mull over the things that are beyond this world, which contrasts with the worldly concerns of the Output, Wealth, and Power.

Traditionally, the Indirect Resource symbolized a "motherly figure" such as an aunt, step-mother, or a nanny rather than one's real mother, but modern interpretations have moved on to include the mother. Because the Indirect Resource shares the same yin-yang energy with the Day Master, the synergy created is one that enables laser sharp focus (as on the subjects of study or research), patience, and endurance. People with several Indirect Resources in their saju don't give up easily and they excel as artists, writers, educators, counselors, and religious and spiritual leaders. They love to learn, immersing deeply into their fields of interest, even though it may be the road less traveled. The learning usually takes the form of non-traditional methods. An example would be a teacher of meditation choosing to enter a monastery to learn his trade instead of enrolling at a university.

Archetype 10: The Proper Resource

The Proper Resource is an element nurturing the Day Master and has the different yin-yang energy. The Proper Resource refers to the mother proper. It symbolizes scholarship, wisdom, humaneness, compassion, warmth, decency, faith, and comfort. Like the Indirect Resource, the Proper Resource encourages the Day Master to pursue education, artistry, religion, and spirituality, but through traditional and visible means.

An example of a saju with well-developed Proper Resources belongs to Mother Teresa who was born on August 26, 1910. (The hour of birth is unknown.)

Hour	Day	Month	Year
?	癸 *gyeh* yin water	甲 *gahp* yang wood	庚 *kyoung* yang metal
?	亥 *hae* yin water	申 *shin* yang metal	戌 *sool* yang earth

The Day Pillar is entirely comprised of Water, enhancing the strength of the 癸 Gyeh Water Day Master. The 庚 Kyoung Metal (Year Stem) and the 申 Shin Metal (Month Branch)—the two most powerful characters out of the twenty-two Stems and Branches in terms of strength and resolve as yang Metals-—are poised as Proper Resources, abundantly supporting the yin water Day Master. Moreover, the 申 Shin Metal Month Branch and the 戌 Sool Earth Year Branch create the harmonious seasonal/directional combination to create more Metal. Without the 酉 Yoo Metal, this is a partial harmonious merger, but it still presents a strong metal energy, increasing the presence of Resource in the chart. As a result, the 戌 Sool Earth that would have been a Proper Power (a husband) to the Day Master loses its identity as an earth element and changes its role to being a Resource through the harmonious merger.

Given her saju composition, it was not a coincidence that Mother Teresa devoted her life to a religious vocation by taking on the title of "Mother" when she made her final vows. The abundance of Proper Resources (the mother proper) shaped who she was—a motherly figure devoted to spirituality, education, charity and service. The 甲 Gahp Wood (Month Stem) serving as an Output known as the Injurer of Controller to the 癸 Gyeh Water Day Master represents Mother Teresa's teaching and speaking abilities. Drawing from 甲 Gahp Wood's leadership, generosity, and nurturing character, Mother Teresa naturally pursued a career in education in the context of her religious institution.

***

◆ The combination of a Water Day Master supported by a Metal Proper Resource(s) is frequently seen in the saju charts of numerous spiritual leaders and people who are spiritually well developed. Water's natural connection to the transcendental realm and the supporting role of the Proper Resource (Metal, in the case of Water) make this possible.

***

The Relationship among the Ten Archetypes

The bulk of saju interpretation is done by interpreting the positions and the functions of the Ten Archetypes found in the saju chart. To ascertain their effect, it is important to not only understand their relationship with the Day Master, but also their relationship with one another. Their relationships constitute the structural rules that apply to all saju compositions.

Rivalry Nurtures Output

Both Sibling and Stealer of Wealth are nurturers of Eating God and Injurer of Controller. Rivalry can help the Self toward Output, just as one can ask a friend for help with work. This rule applies regardless of the yin-yang energy of the involved characters.

Output Nurtures Wealth

Both Eating God and Injurer of Controller are nurturers of Indirect and Proper Wealths. It makes sense that the more you work (output), the more wealth you will accumulate.

Wealth Nurtures Power

Both Indirect and Proper Wealths are nurturers of Indirect and Proper Powers. It seems convincing that money can buy power.

Power Nurtures Resource

Both Indirect and Proper Powers are nurturers of Indirect and Proper Resources. A Resource can always give help to the Day Master by distracting its controllers — the Power characters — from overly dominating the Self. If the Day Master's suffering is too great due to the presence of Powers, utilizing the Resource characters is a way to neutralize or ease the suffering.

Resource Nurtures Rivalry

Both Indirect and Proper Resources are nurturers of Sibling and Stealers of Wealth. It makes sense that a mother is also the nurturer of the siblings of the Self.

***

There are nurturing relationships and there are challenging (controlling) relationships. The yin and yang always coexist.

***

Rivalry Challenges Wealth

Both Sibling and Stealers of Wealth are challengers of Indirect and Proper Wealths, hence the term, the "Stealer of Wealth." For people with a saju with several Siblings or Stealers of Wealth, safeguarding their wealth can be an issue; it is usually the Self's greed or overconfidence (as well as temptations presented by peers) that causes a financial loss.

Wealth Challenges Resource

Both Indirect and Proper Wealths are challengers of Indirect and Proper Resources. As Wealth represents a "father" and Resource, a "mother," the (traditional) rationale for the Wealth's control over the Resource stands.

Resource Challenges Output

Both Indirect and Proper Resources are challengers of Eating God and Injurer of Controller. For people with several Resource characters in their saju, maintaining a job can be challenging, because they are likely to follow the leisurely instinct of Resource and become too laid-back or even lazy, as they expect a "motherly figure" to come into their life and kindly hand them the resources they need.

Output Challenges Power

Both Eating God and Injurer of Controller are challengers of Indirect and Proper Powers, hence the term, the "Injurer of Controller." When the Output characters are positioned closely to the Power characters, the Power Stems or Branches cannot serve their function properly because they are "injured."

Power Challenges Rivalry

Both Indirect and Proper Powers are challengers of Siblings and Stealers of Wealth, just as they are challengers to the Self.

***

The relationships among the Ten Archetypes follow the relational dynamics of the Five Elements. We are simply adding another layer of terminology to what we already know.

***

Chapter 14 Exercise

1. Examine the archetypes in your saju chart. Are there any overlapping ones? Is there a missing category? The dominant archetypes can be determined when they appear more than once in the chart, or if they occupy the Day and/or the Month Branch. Determine your dominant archetype and explore what that says about you and your life.

Chapter 15 Interpreting the Four Pillars

If you do not change direction, you may end up where you are heading.
Lao Tzu

Interpreting a saju chart entails understanding the composition of the Four Pillars in terms of their natural elements, yin-yang energy, Stem-Branch combinations, and how these individual Stems and Branches interact with each other in the layout as archetypes. How the Larger Luck cycles are lined up to interact with the chart—with the Day Pillar in particular—is also important in forecasting the flow of one's destiny.

The Houses of the Four Pillars

As a philosophical system concerned with the dimension of time, the Four Pillars system assigns four temporal contexts to the exact moment of birth, where a person takes his or her first breath in this world:

The Year Pillar

If a saju is considered as a tree, the Year Pillar symbolizes the root system of the tree. The Year Pillar signifies one's ancestral roots, including the grandparents. It represents the saju owner's life from birth to about 18 years of age. Traditionally, the Year Stem is known as the House of male ancestors and the Year Branch as the House of female ancestors. Some believe that the saju owner's former life can be read from the Year Pillar, but it is likely that those who can perform this task would have a special—spiritual or psychic—ability to do so.

The Month Pillar

The Month Pillar symbolizes the growing sprout of the tree. It represents the saju owner's family of origin, especially the parents. The Month Stem is known as the House of father and the Month Branch as the House of mother; though fathers (Wealth) and mothers (Resource) are not always found in their traditional Houses. The Month Pillar is concerned with the time period of young adulthood, from age 19 to about 29. The Month Branch is considered the second most important character in the saju following the Day Stem (the Self), as it represents the general living environment of the Self.

The Day Pillar

The Day Pillar symbolizes the blossoming flowers on the tree— the prime segment in life. The Day Stem represents the Self, and the Day Branch is known as the House of spouse. The Day Pillar is concerned with the time period between age 30 to about 55. A saju reader is most concerned with the Day Pillar and its well-being during an analysis.

The Hour Pillar

The Hour Pillar symbolizes the fruits of the tree. It represents the fruit of one's labor, including work, children and other descendants. The Hour Stem is known as the House of career (Output) and the Hour Branch as the House of children. The Hour Pillar concerns the time period from age 56 and beyond.

Hour	Day	Month	Year
House of Career/Output	The Self	House of Father	House of Ancestors (Grandfather)
House of Children	House of Spouse	House of Mother	House of Ancestors (Grandmother)
age 56~	age 30~55	age 19~29	age 1~18

The symbolic meaning of each Pillar is important, but the symbols should not be applied rigidly, since the Ten Archetypes are not always found in the Houses in which they belong. If there is a Proper Wealth in the House of spouse in a male chart, we can say that this man is destined to marry a woman without difficulty. But a Wealth character *can* be found in other Pillars and not necessarily in the House of spouse. If a Proper Wealth is found in the Year or the Month Pillar, it can be interpreted as entering marriage at a relatively early age, and/or marrying someone older than the Self. If found in the Hour Pillar, the probability of marrying someone late in life is high. The lifetime segments associated with each Pillar should also be viewed theoretically and not taken literally. A Proper Wealth found in the Year Pillar in a male chart, for instance, does not have to mean that the saju owner will marry as a teenager.

Interpretative information comes in layers in a saju chart. A mindful saju reader is one who is able to combine the layers and delineate a *picture* that stands out as a result. This is similar to the gestalt approach. It is also like practicing alchemy. There are many interactive variables to explore—the eight characters of the Four Pillars, the constantly moving luck cycles in multiple time frames, and the Hidden-Stems-in-Branches that covertly interact with the Day Master.

Hence, each reading should have a focus; working with a limited number of specific questions will yield a more productive interpretation experience. I always ask my clients to bring their questions, and the clients who do this get the most out of the reading session. By choosing your questions, you are actively engaging the inquiry process. The intention, or the purpose brought forth by the client, works like a turn-on switch to activate divination. The heaven and the earth are always ready—to engage your searching mind when you are willing to commit to finding the answers.

The Basic Steps to Interpreting the Four Pillars: A Summary

1. Obtain the accurate birthdate information including the birth hour. Check whether the information is from the lunar or the solar calendar if you need to. It is more convenient to use the solar date without having to be concerned about the leap months of the lunar calendar. Obtain the location of birth (as in city) to calculate the exact hour of birth. Some countries use daylight saving time and some don't.

2. Establish the Four Pillars and the LLCS by checking the TTY calendar, or by using an online saju calculator or a mobile app. In the case of birth hour being unknown, it is possible to analyze just three out of the Four Pillars by leaving the Hour Pillar blank, or by ignoring the Hour Pillar if you had to insert a random hour of birth to access your saju chart.

3. Ascertain the Day Master and the surrounding Stems and Branches. Check for the yin-yang balance, the relational dynamics of the elements, and the positions of the archetypes. Is there any missing archetype? Do some archetypes show up more than once? Check for any mergers or clashes among the Stems and the Branches. Which archetypes are subjected to a merger or a clash? How do these mergers or clashes involving different archetypes translate to the life you have lived or are living?

4. Review the LLCS to see how they support or challenge the saju composition over time, especially in relation to the well-being of the Day Master and the Day Branch. Determine where the Day Master stands in terms of the current time frame specified by the Larger Luck cycle. You can determine this by identifying the archetypes presented by the luck cycles. Does the luck cycle show five

years of an Output, Power, Wealth, Resource, or Rivalry? Do any of the yearly luck cycles overlap with the Larger Luck cycle where a significant Stem or Branch appears repeatedly? Do you recognize the presence of any *shin-sahl* in the chart?

5. Engage the specific questions you (or the querent) have about your life and destiny.

A Study Case: Ideal vs. Reality

The saju chart of Elvis Presley has been selected for the final interpretation exercise in this book. He is a well-known figure as the King of Rock 'n' Roll and the cultural icon of twentieth-century America. Elvis A. Presley was born on January 8, 1935 in Tupelo, Mississippi, in the early morning hours, around 4:35am.

Larger Luck Cycle Sequence

Presley's Day Master is the 甲 Gahp Wood standing on the 申 Shin Metal Day Branch below. As a yang wood and a yang metal combo, the Day Pillar indicates two great energies that are clashing with each other. (Various forms of self-damaging tendency can easily become a part of life with this particular Day Pillar composition.) The Day Pillar conveys an imagery of a large tree standing on a large boulder where the tree really can't root itself. Therefore, "movement" is a critical keyword for this Day Pillar, as the tree's roots are constantly shifting to find a place to settle, but to no avail. For such a tree, it hurts to just stand still with a large piece of rock/metal underneath; but this tree is doing it in style, with an air of solitariness. A tree that grows out of a rock is not only mysterious but also beautiful and peerless.

The 申 Shin Metal Day Branch's animal sign is Monkey, so the imagery of an energetic, skillful monkey speedily climbing up and down the tree also fits with this Day Pillar. (It's an interesting tidbit that Presley had a pet chimpanzee named Scatter.) With the 申 Shin Metal Traveling Horse *shin-sahl* in the Day Pillar, the owner of this saju is destined to travel extensively throughout his life. This was indeed the case with Presley who had done countless tours in North America as a famed rock 'n' roll singer and a movie star. He moved from cities to cities to perform; and he also moved his body during his performances—in an unprecedented manner for his time—to express himself and his art.

The two Output Stems, 丁 Jeong Fire and 丙 Byoung Fire, enveloping the 甲 Gahp Wood Day Master indicate the enormous desire for creative productivity using the voice—singing, in the case of Presley. With an Injurer of Controller (Month Stem) and an Eating God (Hour Stem) that come as yin and yang Fires, the 甲 Gahp Wood Day Master is destined to pursue a career in entertainment, and with much success too, based on the exceptional talent contributed by the two Output Stems. The powerful 甲 Gahp Wood facing the flamboyant 丙 Byoung Fire loves to wield showmanship marked by glamor and magnetism. The 甲 Gahp Wood Day Master is also a natural leader with charisma, and with the Fire element as Output, the charismatic leadership is significantly enhanced. People can't help but notice a large, beautiful tree shining under a bright sun.

Meanwhile, it is the power of 丁 Jeong Fire that is at the center of Presley's inspiration and tenacious search for perfection with his craft. As an Injurer of Controller achieving the yin-yang balance with the Day Master, the 丁 Jeong Fire is poised to melt and shape the 申 Shin Metal Day Branch which, in turn, is breaking and cutting up the 甲 Gahp Wood Day Master, to not only carve it into something useful and beautiful, but also to make firewood to inflame the 丁 Jeong Fire for increased output. This is an ongoing, creative productive cycle rolling at the cost of 甲申 (Gahp-Shin) Day Pillar's self-sacrificial activity.

To find stability, the 甲 Gahp Wood Day Master needs soil to ground itself, and, fortunately, the presence of 丑 Chook Earth and 戌 Sool Earth fulfills this need. The 丑 Chook Earth in the Month Pillar in particular serves an important function as it offers the much-needed Water element, albeit it is a Hidden-Stem of 癸 Gyeh Water situated as the mother proper for the yang wood Day Master. The 丑 Chook Earth, located in the House of mother, is also a Nobleman of Heavens to the 甲 Gahp Wood Day Master, implying a special relationship—or a sense of dependency—Presley had with his mother as an only child. (The identical Sibling of 甲 Gahp Wood in the Year Pillar can be seen as Presley's stillborn twin brother who could have been with Presley in spirit during his lifetime.) The 丑 Chook Earth depicting the industrious, patient ox informs of Presley's strong work ethic. Work comes before anything in life when the hardworking 丑 Chook Earth occupies the Month Branch; and the same can be said about his mother—as this is the House of mother with the mother proper residing in it as a Hidden-Stem.

The 丑 Chook Earth and 戌 Sool Earth in the Month and Year Pillars represent both Indirect and Proper Wealths to the 甲 Gahp Wood Day Master. Presley came from a humble working-class family, but he quickly rose to fame as a young adult and began to accumulate considerable wealth. Wealth representing women in male charts, it is fair to say that Presley never lacked the company of women throughout his life. Not only the strong combination of 丑 Chook Earth and 戌 Sool Earth in the saju guarantees this, but his LLCS also shows that the first 3 decades of his life since age 9 are studded with Wealth characters—with the two Wealth Stems (戌, 己) and one Wealth Branch (辰). The owner of this saju naturally cannot avoid an influx of women and money coming through in life.

There is a catch to this many Wealth characters showing up in the saju chart and in the luck cycles. As an archetype, Wealth is an enervator to the Self. Too many Proper or Indirect Wealths can weaken the Day Master that could result in the decline in health. Moreover, in the case of Presley, the 丑 Chook Earth and 戌 Sool Earth create the partial 丑戌未 Penal Triad, thus increasing the risk of money or relationship problems in the form of betrayal.

Elvis Presley died at a relatively young age of 42. His death occurred during his 5-year luck of 辛 Shin Metal (the first half of the 10-year luck of 辛巳) in the year of 丁巳 Red Snake in 1977. To understand one's death that comes in an abrupt manner, we need to explore the strength of the Day Master in the saju composition. Presley's 甲 Gahp Wood Day Master has two Siblings that give some support to the Self: the 甲 Gahp Wood in the Year Pillar and the 寅 Inn Wood in the Hour Pillar. However, the role of these Siblings is limited, since the 甲 Gahp Wood is not standing next to the Self for full support and the 寅 Inn

Wood is actually clashing with the 申 Shin Metal Day Branch. The rest of the Stems and Branches in the chart come in the forms of Wealth (2), Output (2), and Power (1) that are working to enervate the Self. So, we can say that the Self to Others' ratio is 3:5. In this case, the 甲 Gahp Wood Day Master is deemed weak, even though 甲 Gahp Wood itself is not a weak element as a yang wood.

What the 甲 Gahp Wood Day Master truly needs for support and strength is Resource, a water element. Very little water is found in his saju, as Water only comes as two Hidden-Stems inside the 申 and 丑 Branches. Apparently, the majority of the Hidden-Stems is composed of the elements that constantly enervate the Self: Wealth (4), Power (3), and Output (2). In Presley's case, it would have been ideal to find a good flow of Water that comes through the luck cycles, but this doesn't occur until the singer reaches age 49. If he were alive by then, he could have enjoyed the 2 decades of Larger Luck cycles defined by 壬 Yim Water and 癸 Gyeh Water that would have allowed him to relax and recuperate from the demanding career he had. Unfortunately, his life ended during the 5-year luck of 辛 Shin Metal, a Proper Power luck cycle that most likely pushed the singer to produce beyond his means. Moreover, the year of 丁 巳 was a year of "Output" for Presley, so he could not have stopped working no matter the circumstances. Also in that year, the 巳 Sah Fire merged with both 申 Shin Metal Day Branch and 寅 Inn Wood Hour Branch in his chart to create the perfect 寅巳申 Penal Triad, a powerful *shin-sahl* that can be lethal to a weakened Day Master. Presley faced death in August, a 申 Shin Metal month that had compounded the lethal energy of the 寅 巳申 Penal Triad.

Elvis Presley's saju resembles Michael Jackson's saju, with potent Output Stems surrounding the Day Master who has an Indirect Power (the most challenging archetype to the Self) situated in the Day Branch:

Elvis Presley's Four Pillars				Michael Jackson's Four Pillars			
Hour	Day	Month	Year	Hour	Day	Month	Year
丙	甲	丁	甲	辛	戊	庚	戊
byoung	gahp	jeong	gahp	shin	moo	kyoung	moo
寅	申	丑	戌	酉	寅	申	戌
inn	shin	chook	sool	yoo	inn	shin	sool

Though separated by 24 years, the two superstars were born in the same 戊 Sool Earth Year (a powerful Ornate Palanquin that contributed to their talent and enormous success), and they both have their Day Branch subjected to a 寅申 (Inn-Shin) clash, foreshadowing significant health and intimate relationship problems. Both sajus have plenty of yang energy, yet in the absence of Water—the elemental force in charge of life and longevity. Without even looking at their individual Larger Luck Cycle sequences for comparison, it is obvious that they would share similar successes and troubles in reference to their career and health. The two singers, in fact, shared similar circumstances in which they took their last breaths, forever changing history with their untimely passings.

As a side note, I want to emphasize the uniqueness of each saju for each person. Records indicate that women in the US gave birth to approximately 2.37 million babies in 1935, which, on average, means that 6500 babies were born on Elvis Presley's birthday. When we divide the day into 12 segments (to select the 2-hour block for the Hour Pillar), we can say that about 541 babies share the exact same saju chart with Presley. We know from history that not all these babies turned out to be an entertainment superstar or somebody even close to being as famous as Presley had been—he was the only one. Apart from the saju chart, the babies differed in gender, race, socio-economic context, family lineage and history, and physical appearance—all of which play an important role in shaping one's destiny. This is the reason why a physiognomical reading is often simultaneously administered during a saju consultation. No other person in Presley's time period shared the appearance and the stature of Elvis who looked, moved, and sounded like someone fit to be the King of Rock 'n' Roll.

Afterword

Some time ago, I was approached by a person who appeared to be in a state of panic and confusion, perhaps even anger. She asked a terse question, "Can my saju be changed?" She was apparently reacting to bad news concerning her saju from a number of practitioners she had seen. I answered that one's time of birth and the eight characters that are encoded in the time cannot be changed, but the saju owner may use his or her will power and religious faith to live a better life than what is generally implied in the saju chart. I didn't hear from the person again. She might have thought, "What's the point of consulting a specialist if my destiny is up to me?"

On a different occasion long ago when I was a fledgling saju consultant, I did a reading for a man whose saju was reasonably well balanced with opportunities and potential. This, however, didn't matter to him as he continued to stay negative, focusing on his problems with money and intimate relationships. He was trapped in a reality of discontent, and could not see the world beyond it. My encounter with this particular querent turned out to be a lesson for me, as I had consciously acknowledged that one's saju is more like a roadmap than a blueprint—that the person holding the map has to *do* the traveling, with diligence and humility, and timely understanding of himself and his context. Keeping a positive attitude matters. Self-awareness and patience are golden.

A saju is not so much a blueprint where everything is to happen exactly the way it is designed. The Four Pillars established by the temporal boundaries of our world resemble an organic entity; it longs to command, and be commanded by, its owner. In a way, it is more than a roadmap; it is both the reflection and the influencer of our subconscious. Carl Jung stated, "Until you make the unconscious conscious, it will direct your life and you will call it fate." Your saju offers a roadmap to your subconscious, and in analyzing it, you will see the inner workings of your subconscious that is, one way or another, connected to your future.

There is much more to sajuology than what is presented in this book. In this primer, I have attempted to introduce the discipline in an approachable fashion, with the belief that this unique inquiry concerning our individual destiny can help to enhance and transform the lives of those who inquire. The question about our destiny concerns our past—as in our ancestral and cultural heritage. It also concerns our present that comes with a long list of descriptions defining who and where we are. Exploring your saju involves the moments of reflection into your past and the present, which will help you to delineate the most grounded pathway to your future.

Today, the abstract notion of "future" seems to generate a sense of collective anxiety. This is due to the profound issue of climate change facing our generation of the human race. Considering that sajuology was developed out of the temperate climate regions that come with four beautiful, distinctive seasons throughout the year, its utility may be questioned, if and when we lose sight of the four seasons as a result of the rapidly progressing global climate change. Perhaps it may take hundreds or even thousands of years before this ever happens, but as long as *change* remains *constant*, human destiny as we know it may also change someday.

Appendix A

How to Find the Hour Pillar

The Hour of 子 Jah Water (Hour of Rat, 23:00–00:59) is the first hour of the day. The rest of the 2-hour segments follow the order of the Earthly Branch sequence.

Earthly Branch		Hours of the Day	Time
子	Jah Water	Hour of Rat	23:00 ~ 00:59
丑	Chook Earth	Hour of Ox	01:00 ~ 02:59
寅	Inn Wood	Hour of Tiger	03:00 ~ 04:59
卯	Myo Wood	Hour of Rabbit	05:00 ~ 06:59
辰	Jin Earth	Hour of Dragon	07:00 ~ 08:59
巳	Sah Fire	Hour of Snake	09:00 ~ 10:59
午	Oh Fire	Hour of Horse	11:00 ~ 12:59
未	Mee Earth	Hour of Sheep	13:00 ~ 14:59
申	Shin Metal	Hour of Monkey	15:00 ~ 16:59
酉	Yoo Metal	Hour of Rooster	17:00 ~ 18:59
戌	Sool Earth	Hour of Dog	19:00 ~ 20:59
亥	Hae Water	Hour of Pig	21:00 ~ 22:59

To find the Heavenly Stem for your Hour Pillar, check the Stem occupying your Day Pillar (the Day Master) in the saju. The Hour Pillar Reference Table lists the Hour Pillars that accompany specific sets of Day Stems.

Hour of Day \ Day Stem	甲, 己	乙, 庚	丙, 辛	丁, 壬	戊, 癸
23:00 ~ 00:59	甲子	丙子	戊子	庚子	壬子
01:00 ~ 02:59	乙丑	丁丑	己丑	辛丑	癸丑
03:00 ~ 04:59	丙寅	戊寅	庚寅	壬寅	甲寅
05:00 ~ 06:59	丁卯	己卯	辛卯	癸卯	乙卯
07:00 ~ 08:59	戊辰	庚辰	壬辰	甲辰	丙辰
09:00 ~ 10:59	己巳	辛巳	癸巳	乙巳	丁巳
11:00 ~ 12:59	庚午	壬午	甲午	丙午	戊午
13:00 ~ 14:59	辛未	癸未	乙未	丁未	己未
15:00 ~ 16:59	壬申	甲申	丙申	戊申	庚申
17:00 ~ 18:59	癸酉	乙酉	丁酉	己酉	辛酉
19:00 ~ 20:59	甲戌	丙戌	戊戌	庚戌	壬戌
21:00 ~ 22:59	乙亥	丁亥	己亥	辛亥	癸亥

The Hour Pillar Reference Table

The 2-hour segments use the same Earthly Branch throughout the row, indicating the actual time of the day. However, the Heavenly Stems change according to the Day Stem in the saju chart. The 甲 and 己 Day Stems use the Hour Pillars on the first column; the 乙 and 庚 Day Stems use the Hour Pillars on the second column, and so on. Notice that the Stems are moving down the columns in their natural order, and continuing and repeating their sequence in the next column. If your Day Master (Day Stem) is 壬 Yim Water, for instance, and you were born at 6pm, you will use 己酉 as your Hour Pillar as shown in the fourth column. (Subtract one hour from your birth hour before constructing your Hour Pillar if your time of birth falls in daylight saving time.)

Appendix B

The Sexagenary Cycle and the *Gongmang* Pairs

The Sexagenary Cycle										Leftover Branches
甲子 1	乙丑 2	丙寅 3	丁卯 4	戊辰 5	己巳 6	庚午 7	辛未 8	壬申 9	癸酉 10	戌亥 *sool, hae*
甲戌 11	乙亥 12	丙子 13	丁丑 14	戊寅 15	己卯 16	庚辰 17	辛巳 18	壬午 19	癸未 20	申酉 *shin, yoo*
甲申 21	乙酉 22	丙戌 23	丁亥 24	戊子 25	己丑 26	庚寅 27	辛卯 28	壬辰 29	癸巳 30	午未 *oh, mee*
甲午 31	乙未 32	丙申 33	丁酉 34	戊戌 35	己亥 36	庚子 37	辛丑 38	壬寅 39	癸卯 40	辰巳 *jin, sah*
甲辰 41	乙巳 42	丙午 43	丁未 44	戊申 45	己酉 46	庚戌 47	辛亥 48	壬子 49	癸丑 50	寅卯 *inn, myo*
甲寅 51	乙卯 52	丙辰 53	丁巳 54	戊午 55	己未 56	庚申 57	辛酉 58	壬戌 59	癸亥 60	子丑 *jah, chook*

1. If your Day Pillar is found in the first row, your *gongmang* pair is 戌亥.
2. If your Day Pillar is found in the second row, your *gongmang* pair is 申酉.
3. If your Day Pillar is found in the third row, your *gongmang* pair is 午未.
4. If your Day Pillar is found in the fourth row, your *gongmang* pair is 辰巳.

5. If your Day Pillar is found in the fifth row, your *gongmang* pair is 寅卯.

6. If your Day Pillar is found in the sixth row, your *gongmang* pair is 子丑.

Appendix C

The Hidden-Stems-in-Branches Table

Branch Months	Hidden Stems	Beginning Period		Middle Period		Beginning Period	
寅	February	戊	7 days	丙	7 days	甲	16 days
卯	March	甲	10 days			乙	20 days
辰	April	乙	9 days	癸	3 days	戊	18 days
巳	May	戊	7 days	庚	7 days	丙	16 days
午	June	丙	10 days	己	9 days	丁	11 days
未	July	丁	9 days	乙	3 days	己	18 days
申	August	戊	7 days	壬	7 days	庚	16 days
酉	September	庚	10 days			辛	20 days
戌	October	辛	9 days	丁	3 days	戊	18 days
亥	November	戊	7 days	甲	7 days	壬	16 days
子	December	壬	10 days			癸	20 days
丑	January	癸	9 days	辛	3 days	己	18 days

O-BOOKS

SPIRITUALITY

O is a symbol of the world, of oneness and unity; this eye represents knowledge and insight. We publish titles on general spirituality and living a spiritual life. We aim to inform and help you on your own journey in this life.
If you have enjoyed this book, why not tell other readers by posting a review on your preferred book site?

Recent bestsellers from O-Books are:

Heart of Tantric Sex
Diana Richardson
Revealing Eastern secrets of deep love and intimacy to Western couples.
Paperback: 978-1-90381-637-0 ebook: 978-1-84694-637-0

Crystal Prescriptions
The A-Z guide to over 1,200 symptoms and their healing crystals
Judy Hall
The first in the popular series of eight books, this handy little guide is packed as tight as a pill bottle with crystal remedies for ailments.
Paperback: 978-1-90504-740-6 ebook: 978-1-84694-629-5

Shine On
David Ditchfield and J S Jones
What if the aftereffects of a near-death experience were undeniable? What if a person could suddenly produce high-quality paintings of the afterlife, or if they acquired the ability to compose classical symphonies? Meet: David Ditchfield.
Paperback: 978-1-78904-365-5 ebook: 978-1-78904-366-2

The Way of Reiki
The Inner Teachings of Mikao Usui
Frans Stiene
The roadmap for deepening your understanding of the system of Reiki and rediscovering your True Self.
Paperback: 978-1-78535-665-0 ebook: 978-1-78535-744-2

You Are Not Your Thoughts.
Frances Trussell
The journey to a mindful way of being, for those who want to truly know the power of mindfulness.
Paperback: 978-1-78535-816-6 ebook: 978-1-78535-817-3

The Mysteries of the Twelfth Astrological House
Fallen Angels
Carmen Turner-Schott, MSW, LISW
Everyone wants to know more about the most misunderstood house in astrology — the twelfth astrological house.
Paperback: 978-1-78099-343-0 ebook: 978-1-78099-344-7

WhatsApps from Heaven
Louise Hamlin
An account of a bereavement and the extraordinary signs — including WhatsApps — that a retired law lecturer received from her deceased husband.
Paperback: 978-1-78904-947-3 ebook: 978-1-78904-948-0

The Holistic Guide to Your Health & Wellbeing Today
Oliver Rolfe
A holistic guide to improving your complete health,
both inside and out.
Paperback: 978-1-78535-392-5 ebook: 978-1-78535-393-2

Cool Sex
Diana Richardson and Wendy Doeleman
For deeply satisfying sex, the real secret is to reduce
the heat, to cool down. Discover the empowerment
and fulfilment of sex with loving mindfulness.
Paperback: 978-1-78904-351-8 ebook: 978-1-78904-352-5

Creating Real Happiness A to Z
Stephani Grace
Creating Real Happiness A to Z will help you understand
the truth that you are not your ego
(conditioned self).
Paperback: 978-1-78904-951-0 ebook: 978-1-78904-952-7

A Colourful Dose of Optimism
Jules Standish
It's time for us to look on the bright side, by boosting
our mood and lifting our spirit, both in our interiors,
as well as in our closet.
Paperback: 978-1-78904-927-5 ebook: 978-1-78904-928-2

Readers of ebooks can buy or view any of
these bestsellers by
clicking on the live link in the title. Most titles
are published in paperback and as an ebook.
Paperbacks are available in traditional bookshops.
Both print and ebook formats are available online.

Find more titles and sign up to our readers' newsletter at
www.o-books.com
Follow O books on Facebook at **O-books**

For video content, author interviews and more, please subscribe to our YouTube channel:

O-BOOKS Presents

Follow us on social media for book news, promotions and more:

Facebook: O-Books

Instagram: @o_books_mbs

Twitter: @obooks

Tik Tok: @ObooksMBS

www.o-books.com